Stockwell Depot 1967–79

John Fowler, Roelof Louw, Gerard Hemsworth, David Evison, Roger Fagin, Roland Brener and Peter Hide, Stockwell Depot, London, 1968 (clockwise from back left)

Sam Cornish

Stockwell Depot 1967–79

with interviews by Sam Cornish
and David Waterworth

Ridinghouse
University of Greenwich

Exterior of Stockwell Depot, London, May 1971

Contents

Preface

Schematic histories of sculpture are often structured around moments of change. Groundbreaking group exhibitions, for example, can mark endings, as well as pointing to new beginnings. What happens in between such caesura moments can often become neglected or even forgotten.

Sculpture in Britain between the mid-1960s and early 1980s – between influential exhibitions such as *The New Generation: 1965* at the Whitechapel Art Gallery, London in 1965 and *Objects & Sculpture* at the Institute of Contemporary Arts (ICA), London and Arnolfini, Bristol in 1981 – has, broadly speaking, suffered from such art historical neglect. This situation is gradually changing: the 1970s are now being considered as a fascinating decade for sculpture – full of experimentation, cross-disciplinary activity and critical contestation. The activity at Stockwell Depot sits squarely within this period, and for a number of years now it has come to stand for the heavy, welded, metal sculpture that emerged from St Martin's School of Art, London in the late 1960s and throughout the 1970s from the leading example of Anthony Caro's work and its followers. Indeed, the phrase Stockwell Sculpture has often been used synonymously with Stockwell Depot. Whilst this new publication accounts for this idea – highlighting the roles, motivations and contributions of key artists including Roland Brener, David Evison, John Foster, Katherine Gili, Peter Hide and Anthony Smart – it also enables a better understanding of the complex history of Stockwell Depot: its contested identity and function; its changing cast of tenants; its exhibitions and the differing (and often conflicting) concerns of the artists associated with it. It was a place of reaction as much as absorption; of experimentation as much as emulation.

Through this new research, conducted by Sam Cornish, we learn that a large number of artists exhibited, rented or worked in spaces at Stockwell Depot – most prominently between 1967 and 1979 – although the building was used as a studio and occasional exhibition space until its eventual closure in 1993. The artists involved with Stockwell Depot include sculptors and painters, men and women, well-known figures and lesser-known artists. Whilst St Martin's was the dominant art school with which they were affiliated, other schools and colleges had a presence as well. Looking back, 'Who were Stockwell Depot?' is as valid and valuable a question to ask as 'What was Stockwell Depot?'

Working outside the art school was a crucial part of Stockwell Depot's early *raison d'être*; it offered not only larger spaces for the production, display and storage of sculpture, but also afforded a space for critical and institutional independence in which ideas could be tried and tested in a supportive, artistic environment. As Cornish's text demonstrates, this former brewery on Combermere Road was a building with a real physicality, a material weight and a rough historical patina all of its own – which artists worked with and against. This characterful architecture housed and enhanced not just the art made within it, but also the critical reception itself. Caro and Clement Greenberg were both visitors as well as the dealer Nigel Greenwood, who appreciated the opportunity to view work in such a large, industrial, non-gallery space. Exhibitions were held annually between 1968 and 1979, during which time the Depot provided an intriguing and influential model of a combined studio and exhibition space which other organisations and studio complexes went on to employ and develop.

There are important lessons, still today, to be learned from Stockwell Depot and from how artistic groups and communities interact and work through their ideas in the face of pressures from both outside and within. This timely publication gives access to this, as well as providing a valuable art-historical insight into the fate and fortunes of abstract sculpture in Britain.

Jon Wood
Henry Moore Institute

Installation view, *Stockwell Depot: Sculpture Exhibition*, Stockwell Depot, London, 1968 with Peter Hide, *Sculpture Number 2* (1968)

Beyond the End of Modern Sculpture: Stockwell Depot 1967–79

Sam Cornish

In the summer of 1967, the Stockwell Depot, a former brewery in south London, was converted into studio space by a group of young artists, almost all of them sculptors associated with St Martin's School of Art, London. In May 1968 they held their first studio exhibition. These exhibitions became known as the 'Stockwell Depot Annuals' – continuing until 1979 – and the studios were occupied until the early 1990s. The Depot stands at the very beginning of the rapidly growing phenomenon of artists grouping together to use London's large stock of abandoned buildings as studio space. What distinguished the Stockwell studios from the similarly large, gloomy and draughty brick and steel spaces that followed – warehouses, schools, dock buildings and churches – was its sense of purpose, its dedication to the communal project of modernist abstraction. The Depot's annual exhibitions began at a moment when the assumptions of high modernism were being widely disputed; continuing through a period when many artists and critics thought these assumptions had passed into irrelevance. At the Depot, a succession of young artists were working in and against a changing tide, making art in a 'bleak', 'forbidding' building that provided the setting for an especially late modernism to play itself out.

The Depot was primarily a sculpture studio. Painters worked there throughout its existence, but even when painting became an important part of the Depot exhibitions, those artists involved did not – for the most part – have studios there. Close connections to St Martin's also meant that it was in relation to sculpture that the Depot's contribution was most coherent, complex and ambitious. The sculpture made at Stockwell should be understood in relation to the attitudes that had coalesced at St Martin's during the 1960s. During that decade, the department had established an international reputation as a radical centre for modern sculpture, led by Anthony Caro and the diverse group of sculptors who studied and taught there, now known as the New Generation after an exhibition at the Whitechapel Art Gallery, London, in 1965.[1] Often brightly coloured, in steel or fibreglass, the abstract sculpture produced in and around St Martin's in the 1960s is a key episode in the history of modernism in Britain. Until at least the early 1980s, work in the department was sustained by a belief that it was the place from where the present and the future of sculpture would spring. Grasping this sense of importance – of acting on a world stage, and of acting to further not just individual careers, but the future of the discipline – is crucial to understanding sculpture at Stockwell.

Toward the end of the 1960s, diverse winds of change – from Minimalism and Arte Povera, through to what became known as the 'expanded field' – blew through modernist attitudes and aesthetics. In the Depot's first few years, the spatial extension, succinct and ambiguous objects and colour of New Generation sculpture existed alongside – or sometimes merged with – more self-consciously radical approaches; great importance was placed on a sculpture's interaction with its environment, and new levels of visual severity or reduction were reached. From around 1972 or 1973, sculptors at the Depot began to question the achievements of the New Generation, not because their definition of sculpture had been too restrictive, but because it was too permissive and invaded by disciplines – primarily painting – which were not considered 'proper to sculpture'.[2] The increasingly heavy steel sculpture that developed, which was widely known as Stockwell Sculpture, attained some prestige and limited institutional backing in the 1970s, and then quickly disappeared from view. Even in its brief heyday, Stockwell Sculpture was widely disliked and misunderstood. It is a moment in recent British art history in need of reappraisal.

Not all of the sculptors at the Depot were involved in the tightly knit arguments about the nature of sculpture, which were essential to the development of Stockwell Sculpture: David Evison, in particular, worked an independent furrow. Stockwell Painting had its own narrative, bound up with changing attitudes to American painting stemming from Abstract Expressionism. An account of Stockwell is further complicated by the fact that not all the artists who showed at the annual Depot exhibitions had studios there, nor were all the artists who did have studios necessarily included. The Depot exhibitions were distinctly not open studios – as became popular in Wapping, Stepney or Butler's Wharf – in which artists tidied up their own spaces and opened the doors to the public. By the mid-1970s the exhibitions were hung and selected by a self-appointed – if fairly informal – committee which was as concerned with putting across a particular attitude to painting and sculpture as it was in representing the art made at the Depot. This process may now

1 Six of the nine sculptors in *The New Generation: 1965*, Whitechapel Art Gallery, London had studied at St Martin's: David Annesley, Michael Bolus, Phillip King, Tim Scott, William Tucker and Isaac Witkin. In this essay, the New Generation refers to both Caro and the St Martin's sculptors included in this exhibition.

2 Alan Gouk, 'Proper to Sculpture', lecture, Wimbledon School of Art, January 1980, published in *Artscribe*, no.25, October 1980.

seem partial or nepotistic, but the selection and the competition it entailed are undoubtedly part of what made the Depot a distinctive part of London's scene in the 1970s, and what makes it worth shining light on this almost completely forgotten moment.

Setting up the Depot

Roland Brener, a South African who had emigrated to the United Kingdom because of opposition to Apartheid, was instrumental in setting up Stockwell Depot.[3] Brener had studied at St Martin's in the mid-1960s before returning there to teach, as was common in the department. Approaching the end of his time as a student, he became increasingly conscious that he needed to secure a studio space for when he left. A 'slum room in Whitechapel' shared with Roger Fagin (also a South African, who too had studied, then taught, at St Martin's) was too small for the large sculptures they were making. Living in Clapham, just west of Stockwell, they decided to contact Lambeth Borough Council which eventually suggested the Depot, a building with just over 5,000 square metres of space, and therefore significantly larger than the St Martin's sculpture department.

There had been a brewery on Combermere Road at least as early as 1834; one of two in Stockwell Green that used natural springs as water-sources. Stockwell was then in rural Surrey, and the brewery would have looked out onto fields. Around the middle of the nineteenth century it came into the possession of two brothers, Edward and Thomas Waltham, in time for the speculative housing boom which followed the extension of the railways to Brixton in the 1860s. They owned the site – known as both the 'British Brewery' and the 'Waltham Brothers Brewery' – until the first decade of the twentieth century. In 1908 the building was bought by the Lion Brewery, passing shortly afterwards into the possession of the council. When the artists moved in the council still used parts of the Depot; buses and ambulances were parked in the former Waltham Brothers yard, and some of the ground-floor rooms bordering Combermere Road were used to store items removed from house clearances. Other spaces on the ground floor were let to private businesses.

3 Frank Martin, head of St Martin's sculpture department from 1952–79, claimed that the department set up Stockwell and later Greenwich Studios as 'satellite areas'. See Frank Martin, Artists' Lives interview, British Library. This account is, however, denied by Peter Hide (from Stockwell Depot) and Jeff Lowe (from Greenwich Studios), and likely contains an element of exaggeration on Martin's part.

The sculptors took over rooms on the first and second floors, some in the main mid-Victorian building, and others in what was perhaps a later, but still Victorian, addition, 'The Annexe'. A small blue door on the edge of the imposing facade of the main building on Combermere Road opened to a stairwell, dimly and artificially lit. A section of the metal stairs up to the first floor could be removed, enabling materials to be brought in by hoisting them up the stairwell. Some people stepped with trepidation, uncertain as to whether the stairs had been properly reassembled.

The stairs made a return halfway up. At the top, a turn to the right led into The Annexe and a corridor – on its left were a group of small rooms, possibly former offices, which looked out on to Combermere Road; on the right was a single larger space. Like many of the other spaces this was later subdivided. A left turn at the top of the stairs led to a long room in the older part of the building, whose windows faced the road; bisected by a line of cast-iron columns, it was later known as the 'Pillar Room'. At its far end was the 'Pigeon Room', a derelict part of the brewery where all the floors had been removed or had rotted away, leaving a network of beams – heavily matted with guano – that stank in the summer. A ladder in the Pillar Room provided access through a trapdoor to a room with the same footprint on the floor above. This 'Upper Pillar Room' was crossed laterally by wooden beams, above which ran a raised walkway, and in later years was equipped with a mezzanine level. Staying on the first floor, a door in the Pillar Room opened to the largest single space, which in turn led on to another large room with an exposed ceiling crisscrossed by thin metal beams. This room bordered a large flat roof, and was afforded only meagre protection from the elements by an open steel screen. Somewhat optimistically described as a 'Loggia', the brewery had stabled horses here, which had been led up by a ramp that ran down from the roof. When standing on the roof you could see the arched windows of Stockwell Congregational Church and look out across the sprawl of south London.

Brener and Fagin moved into the Depot in June or July 1967 and thereafter the Depot was occupied in piecemeal fashion, with different areas leased separately from the council. Some parts – most notably the Loggia and the large space next to it – were not included in the original agreements with the council and at first were used rent-free. By the summer of 1968 the Depot was divided into three tenancies: Brener was the principal

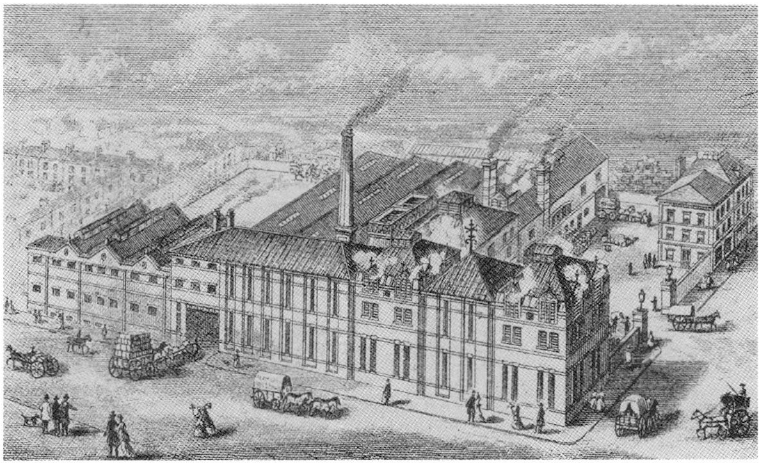

Detail of Waltham Brothers Brewery billhead, 1899

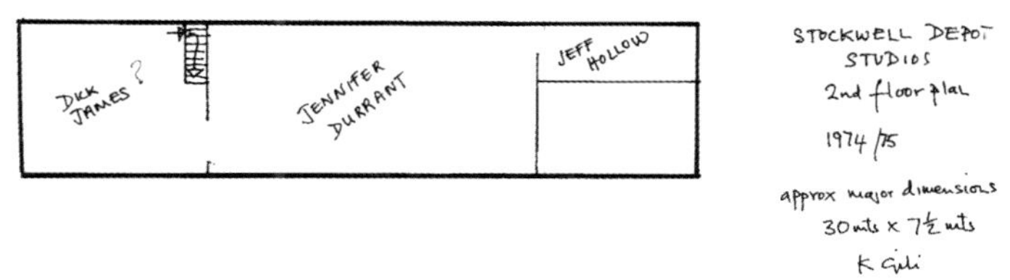

Floor plans of studios at Stockwell Depot, London, drawn from memory by David Evison (The Annexe, below) and Katherine Gili (main area, right)

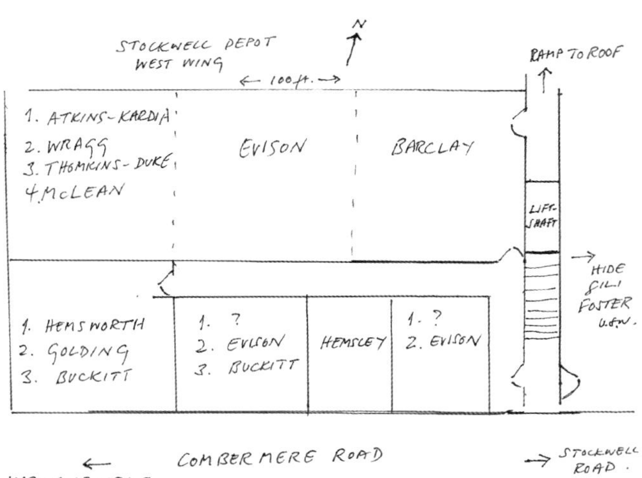

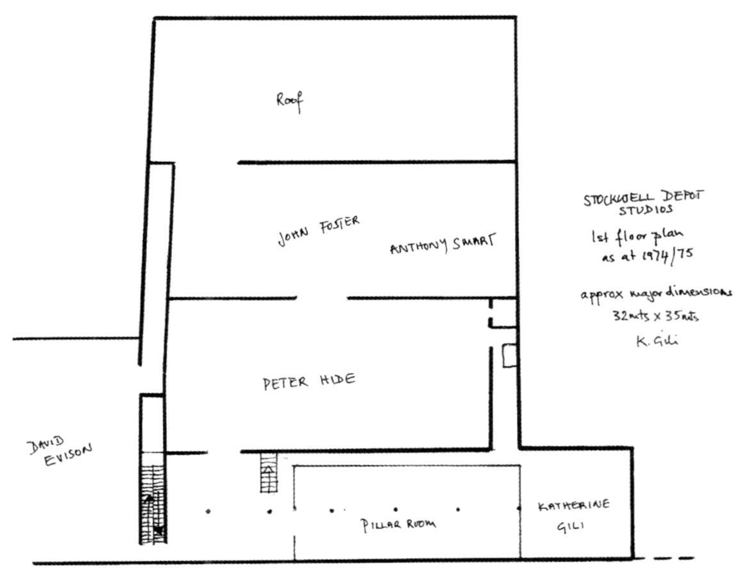

tenant of the Pillar Room, David Evison of the large space in The Annexe, and Gerard Hemsworth of the smaller rooms on the opposite side of the corridor to Evison.[4] To afford the rent, the principal tenants sublet to others, all of whom were associated with St Martin's. Peter Hide moved into Brener's section in August 1967. Working in the Loggia was Roelof Louw, another South African, who, in his early thirties, was seven or eight years older than most of the others. Shirley Cameron was invited by Brener, and moved in over the summer of 1967. The only other woman, and only painter, was Rita Marshall. Peter Atkins (later Kardia), an important and controversial tutor at St Martin's in the late 1960s and 70s and who later set up the influential Environmental Media Department at the Royal College of Art, let a third of Evison's space for a year, but almost never used it. Barry Martin briefly had a space in Hemsworth's area. Andrew Dunlop, who commuted north to teach in Derby while at Stockwell, moved in at the beginning of 1968. Alan Barkley and John Fowler were among the last of the initial group to join, moving into The Annexe in the spring of 1968.

Between the New Generation and the end of modern sculpture

The first exhibition at Stockwell Depot opened towards the end of May 1968, with sculpture by Barkley, Brener, Evison, Fagin, Fowler, Hemsworth, Hide and Louw. Dunlop and Marshall were not included, nor was Cameron, who subsequently left the Depot as a consequence. The exhibition text stressed that the artists were 'self-selected, form no group and have no common style'. Independent of each other, they also desired to operate outside the commercial imperatives of dealers and the 'judgments of critics, juries and museums' – all of which 'have nothing to do with the direct confrontation of the work and the viewer'. The artists claimed to be united only in relation to the building itself, where 'generous space and the roughness of walls and floors, like relics of old uses, emphasise the physical rather than the visual quality that many of the sculptures have'.[5]

Fire regulations meant that the public was not officially allowed in, although Brener's flair for networking, combined with the prestige of St Martin's and the novelty of the venue, ensured the exhibition was well attended.[6] A week or so before the opening, he appeared (for the second time) on BBC2's discussion programme *Late Night Line-Up*, along with Hide, to talk about the exhibition.[7] The Depot exhibition was novel enough to attract notice in the gossip columns. The *Evening Standard*'s 'Londoner's Diary' observed that, 'Stockwell is no dream palace… the building is like a set for the final scene in a forties thriller' and had Fagin declaring that, 'the whole [Bond Street gallery] system is archaic and hopelessly out of touch with the way sculpture has changed.'[8] David Clemens's column 'Scene' in the *Daily Mirror* quoted a similarly defiant Brener:

> I hope our sculptures aren't essentially visual. They are physical experiences, for walking in, through and round. We want to create new values. We don't make things readily accessible to the art market. We try to create things which people in time might come to accept.[9]

Even more serious critics were as interested in the building as the sculpture it contained. Many almost neglected to mention the sculpture at all; others saw an oppositional or a sympathetic interaction between the work and its surroundings. Guy Brett felt 'each area [in the Depot] is so much raw material for a sculptor who makes open and extended structures', and praised Brener and Louw for 'working with the most originality and perhaps with the freshest response to these rough empty spaces'.[10] Norbert Lynton, a critic and curator less committed than Brett to modernism's avant-garde edge, proposed Stockwell's occupation of disused premises as a solution to the problems caused by sculptors working on an ever-increasing scale, and observed that, 'the structural drama of the building itself offers… strong

4 A note in the Arts Council archive from 8 July 1968 states that Brener and Hemsworth each paid £410 rent and rates per annum, and Evison paid £613.

5 Michael Compton, introduction, *Stockwell Depot: Sculpture Exhibition*, exhibition pamphlet, Stockwell Depot, London, 1968, n.p.

6 Even at this early stage the work produced at Stockwell was gaining attention. At the 1968 exhibition a large outdoor piece by Brener was commissioned for Cécile de Rothschild's French mansion and the *New York Times* dance critic, Don McDonagh, commissioned a work for his Harlem brownstone. Californian collector Ruth Schaffner bought work by Brener and Hide at the 1969 exhibition, and later bought paintings by Richard James.

7 Brener and Hide appeared on *Late Night Line-Up* on 16 May 1968. Brener, along with Fagin, Barry Flanagan and Ian Spencer, previously appeared on the programme on 11 November 1967 to discuss a documentary on Henry Moore.

8 'Londoner's Diary', *Evening Standard*, 29 May 1968.

9 David Clemens, 'Scene', *Daily Mirror*, 28 May 1968.

10 Guy Brett, 'Eight young sculptors at a warehouse', *The Times*, 12 June 1968.

11 Norbert Lynton, 'Magna Opera', *The Guardian*, 8 June 1968.

competition, but most of the sculptures stand up well to it.'[11]

Terser opinion was offered by leading American critic Clement Greenberg, who was invited to the Depot by Caro before the exhibition opened. Greenberg praised Evison's work, but confessed that Brener's lay outside his critical faculties. Hide's *Sculpture Number 2* (1968; pp.10–11) was condemned with the line: 'Too Caro, rigorous geometry doesn't make rigorous art!', while Louw's *Ring II* (1968) was afforded a kick, and a mumbled, 'Fuck American symmetry'. Gerard Hemsworth missed Greenberg's visit, but was told it was brief to the point of dismissal.[12] Greenberg was most associated with the promotion of Abstract Expressionism and its progeny; by the 1960s this had formed an international style, of which painting at the Depot was a regional outpost. Greenberg was also an important supporter of Caro, and to a lesser degree of the New Generation sculptors in general. There was a lack of British critics who shared Greenberg's engagement with modernist abstraction, and none with his influence, so he continued to be an important figure to many at the Depot. He became a regular visitor, and was in turn visited in New York by some of the Stockwell artists.

The success of St Martin's in the 1960s was based upon an intense questioning of what sort of object an abstract sculpture could be – a process particularly associated with its non-accredited postgraduate Advanced Course, which most of the sculptors at Stockwell went through.[13] In the second half of the decade, the New Generation's conclusions began to be disputed by many younger artists at St Martin's, a process which, to an extent, was encouraged by the department itself. This questioning was an important element of wider debates that took place internationally; all at once – although without the rigid categories they have since been divided into – modernist abstraction was beset by Minimalism, post-Minimalism, Arte Povera, Performance art and Conceptualism. The challenges were, by their nature, diverse and contradictory, but many involved a removal of the object from the centre of sculptural inquiry. At this point of crisis the 'idea of the end of modern sculpture' became common currency.[14] There was an increased attention to an object's interaction with, or manipulation of, its surroundings: sculptures could become temporary, or they could exist as an idea or a set of instructions, while activities and things with their own pre-existing identity could be claimed as sculpture. The large spaces of the Depot contained – or enabled – a unique response to this upheaval. Based on the attitudes of the New Generation, many of the artists at the Depot pushed past the limits of sculpture that their teachers had established, facing the new ideas head-on, while still maintaining what Elizabeth C Baker called a 'persistent physicality'.[15]

Using non-art materials such as steel or fibreglass, taking sculpture off the plinth and using open – often laterally spreading – structures, the New Generation had moved sculpture into closer contact with the everyday world. Yet, crucially, they maintained a connection to an older conception of the art form: one still considered as a singular, illusionistic, formally integrated and enduring physical structure, separate from its surroundings, and which the viewer stood outside of. Perhaps paradoxically, the New Generation looked to painting (and to a lesser extent architecture) to maintain this connection, for conformation of sculpture's autonomy, its discrete and coherent existence. Their sculptures were often frontal or resolved around a plane, a manner that came to be called pictorial; or the works involved an equivocally closed volume, which replaced the mass-to-surface relation of traditional figurative sculpture with volumes interrupted with flat surfaces, and so treated as hollow or artificial. Colour suggested a superficial link to Pop art and despite fundamental differences, there was a deeper shared attachment to an ambiguous clarity, sheer untouchable surfaces, and a suppressed Surrealism. There was also a sense of weightlessness, particularly associated with Caro's 'relational' sculpture, though reaching in a crescendo in his and Tim Scott's sculpture of the late 1960s.[16]

Over the course of the first two exhibitions, Barkley, Evison and Fowler remained closest to the New Generation, with Evison able to do so with particular originality. Elements of the strangely tilted quasi-architectural sculptures that Evison showed in the first exhibition can be seen reflected in Caro's work a few years later, while the tall sculptures in the second exhibition –

12 Louw remembered that Greenberg's comment 'drove me to think hard about what I was doing… the work we did was now out in the public domain'. Roelof Louw, email to the author, 17 March 2009.

13 A prior qualification was not a requirement for entry to the Advanced Course, and many professional sculptors enrolled upon it. In the 1960s it was known as the Vocational Course.

14 Raymond J Williams, *After Modern Sculpture: Art in the United States and Europe 1965–1970*, Manchester University Press, Manchester, 2000, p.1.

15 Elizabeth C Baker, 'Traveling Ideas: Germany, England', *ARTnews*, vol.69, no.4, summer 1970, p.71.

16 See Clement Greenberg, 'Anthony Caro' (1965), republished in Richard Whelan (ed), *Anthony Caro*, Penguin Books, London, 1974.

particularly *Flag Sculpture* (1969; p.55) – were a confident response to the New Generation's tendency to horizontal organisation, and look forward to his later work.[17] Hide hesitated between continuation and rejection of his predecessors' example; Hemsworth and Fagin moved from the ideas of their teachers in the first exhibition to sculpture that was pointedly not that by the time of the second exhibition. Some of the Stockwell artists had worked as assistants to the New Generation, and the particular influence of their teacher-employers can be seen in their sculpture: Hide followed Caro's laterally extended steel constructions; Fowler worked out from Phillip King's playful, near-baroque fibreglass curves; and Hemsworth channelled William Tucker's basic or reductive forms. The sculpture of Brener and Louw can be paired off in similar fashion: Brener with Caro and Louw with Tucker.[18] But at the same time their work appears more confident than their peers, offering a synthesis of New Generation sculpture with the ideas that were challenging some of its underlying propositions.

Most of the distinctions between the early work at Stockwell and the New Generation can be extrapolated from the preference for the physical over the visual. On the one hand this involved sculptures becoming environmental, either allowing direct physical involvement or emphasising that they were inextricably part of the situation they were encountered in. On the other, it entailed an increased attention to materiality and the downgrading or rejection of illusionistic effects.

For sculptures to become environmental, they had to break – or at least loosen – the connection New Generation sculpture had made to an older sense of sculpture's identity. In doing so they had to throw off the pictorialism which the New Generation had used to maintain this connection. Viewers had to stand outside Evison's architectural structures (as they did with the architectural sculptures of Caro or Tucker) but were encouraged to enter Brener's, which he felt served as a 'bland structure articulating space… a vehicle for the imposed conceptual demands or imagination of the viewer (participant)'.[19] Art critic Edwin Mullins described himself clambering over the large 'tank-trap' assemblage Fagin showed in the second exhibition – something he would not have thought to do with the Caroesque sculpture Fagin had showed a year earlier.[20] Brener was increasingly concerned with using the minimum amount of material to 'fill large areas of formal space dramatically, in a visual sense'; something that also applied (though with less stress on the drama) to the rope Louw hung from the beams in the Loggia in the second exhibition.[21] Louw's work from the first exhibition comprised building or industrial materials in implicitly contingent and temporary arrangements; as did the drifts of planks in Hemsworth's work in the second. These sculptures became environmental because they implied that they only existed for the duration of the exhibition, and because their coherences did not derive from a set of internal relations but in response to their surroundings. The Depot encouraged these experiments because it allowed sculpture to be shown in the place it was made: there was no need for sculpture to sustain an immutable identity on the journey from studio to gallery. Brener thought much of his work did not make sense when shown elsewhere and he felt 'confident only about using particular space'.[22]

The clearest expression of the 'crisis of modernism' or the 'end of modern sculpture', came with the essay 'Art and Objecthood', published by (the then Greenberg acolyte) Michael Fried in *Artforum* in the summer of 1967 – the moment the Depot was first occupied.[23] The core of Fried's argument was dialectical: modernism's power came from its ability to embrace the tendencies within modern culture that threatened to swamp it. Likewise, modernist sculpture's intensity grew as it became at once more like an everyday object and more like the antithesis of an everyday object – that is, a sculpture. A fear of

17 Evison has suggested that Brener thought that Caro's *Prairie* (1967) was partly based upon some of Brener's sculpture. Similarly, Evison thinks that Caro's *Deep North* (1969–70) drew upon the sculptures Evison exhibited in the *Stockwell 2* exhibition in 1969. Evison's 1968 sculptures are perhaps more obviously echoed in Caro's *Up Front* (1971); while Caro's Racks series (1971–74) could be seen to follow the clear horizontals and diagonals of Hide's sculptures that were shown at Stockwell between 1970–72. The question of Caro's use of his pupils' sculpture in this way is one which deserves further exploration.

18 Louw and Brener were selected by Tucker and Caro respectively for a 1967 group exhibition at Kasmin Limited, London. For more on Brener's close but difficult relation to Caro, see Sarah Milroy, 'A Very Canadian Story: Mowry Baden and Roland Brener in Victoria', *Mowry Baden and Roland Brener: Thirty Years in Victoria*, exhibition catalogue, Art Gallery of Greater Victoria, Victoria, 2006, pp.39–42.

19 Alan Barkley, Roland Brener, David Evison, Roger Fagin, Gerard Hemsworth, Peter Hide and Roelof Louw, 'Sculptors at Stockwell Depot', *Studio International*, vol.177, no.907, January 1969, p.34.

20 Edwin Mullins, 'The Sleeper Awakes', *The Sunday Telegraph*, 5 October 1969.

21 Roland Brener and Peter Hide, 'Roland Brener and Peter Hide – a written discussion', *Studio International*, vol.180, no.925, September 1970, pp.96–97.

22 Roland Brener, statement, 1969, Tate archive.

23 Michael Fried, 'Art and Objecthood', *Artforum*, summer 1967. Fried taught at St Martin's in the early 1970s. In his tribute at the memorial for Caro, held at Tate Britain, London in February 2014, Fried mentioned Brener and Hide amongst some of Caro's prominent pupils.

the breaking of this refinement – so that sculpture and object became indistinguishable, thus rendering art redundant – lay behind the near apocalyptic terms with which Fried pitted New York Minimalism against modernist abstraction, partly in the guise of Caro. That their teacher was accorded such a significant role in Fried's narrative may have caused some of the younger artists chaffing under his influence to switch to the other side. However, it is important to recognise that though Fried's text may have compellingly described and added frisson to the situation, it did not create it: neither Brener nor Louw were the products of New York criticism. Though their sculpture shares much with Minimalism, it moved towards the environmental on its own terms, rooted in the spatial extension of the New Generation. Brener in particular can be seen to attempt such a reconciliation.[24]

What Hide now calls 'structural literalism' was a widespread tendency in British sculpture concerned with the downgrading of illusion. Like Minimalism, it made claim to an increased sense of reality, though it was not reducible to its American cousin. A kind of 'truth to materials', structural literalism entailed creating structure with materials visibly under tension or which in other ways did not disguise – in fact which made manifestly apparent – the mechanics by which a sculpture was constructed. Common to many artists in Britain at the time, it set itself against, and perhaps partly stemmed from, Caro's illusion in which steel components were fixed into relational arrangements with a partial disguising of structure. Caro's sleight of hand was aided by what became known as the 'magic glue' of welding. Connected to the Depot artists' structural literalism, was a gradual rejection of colour and highly finished surfaces in favour of rough surfaces and materials used in their raw state. These attempts to move beyond the premises of the New Generation highlight that in distinction, Evison's originality, for example, was in part an intensification rather than a rejection of New Generation ideas: he tended to increase illusionistic effects rather than suppress them, most clearly through a use of colour which disrupted the underlying structure of his sculptures.

In the summer of 1968, Roger Fagin approached the Arts Council of Great Britain for funding. The response was positive. It was suggested that Stockwell be administered under the aegis of SPACE (Space Provision Artistic Cultural and Educational), which was then in the process of negotiating funding for the studio complex it opened at St Katharine Docks, near Tower Bridge, in 1968 and whose founders – Bridget Riley and Peter Sedgley – had visited Stockwell as part of their research. In the end Stockwell was only a SPACE studio briefly, and then only so on paper. Through the 1970s, SPACE would play a central role in a huge expansion in artists taking over disused buildings to use as studios, though many independent studios followed in Stockwell's footsteps. The Depot received just under £1,000 from the Arts Council between 1968 and 1970, with the first half spent on heating and lighting, and the second on equipment to be used communally. During the 1970s, Stockwell continued to receive occasional funds for equipment and for the maintenance or conversion of spaces, although not at the level of the initial grant. More significant support from the Arts Council came in the form of funding for Depot annuals, grants to individual Depot artists, purchases of artworks and exhibition opportunities.

24 Ray Barrie, who studied at St Martin's and who occasionally worked for Brener as an assistant at Stockwell Depot, emphasised the importance of Caro in this process, suggesting that his abandonment of figuration had created a situation in which 'the real figuration of the living figure (the viewer), can move through and around a newly invented armature.' Ray Barrie, email to the author, 30 September 2014.

Beyond the Depot

By 1970, art critic Caroline Tisdall could suggest that the Depot exhibitions were 'important landmarks for anyone interested in the course of English sculpture'.[25] Depot artists were represented in national and international exhibitions: Hemsworth, Hide and Louw participated in *Survey 68: Abstract Sculpture* at Camden Arts Centre, London (1968);[26] Evison, Hide and Brener were taken by John Kasmin, the most important art dealer in London in the 1960s, to the first Prospect art fair in Dusseldorf; in 1969 Louw was included in *When Attitudes Become Form* at Kunsthalle Bern, Bern and Institute of Contemporary Arts (ICA), London; and Brener was one of the young artists representing Britain at the Sixième Biennale de Paris, Musée d'Art Moderne de la Ville de Paris (1969). Stockwell artists made up the whole of the Arts Council touring exhibition *New Sculpture 1969*. The Depot's prominence was reflected in a *Studio International* magazine special on contemporary British sculpture: amongst various contributions involving Depot artists were Brener's 'The

25 Caroline Tisdall, 'Stockwell Depot: New Sculpture', *The Guardian*, 19 September 1970.

Studios at Stockwell Depot, London, 1971

David Evison

Peter Hide

John Golding

Richard James

Cover of *Stockwell Depot: Eight English Sculptors from London*, exhibition catalogue, Kunstnernes Hus, Oslo, 1970

'The Concerns of Emerging Sculptors' (p.162) and a four-page spread titled, 'Sculptors at Stockwell Depot'.[27] All of this activity, coupled with the fact that exhibiting in a non-traditional space was increasingly fashionable, may well have attracted art dealer Nigel Greenwood, who organised *Stockwell Depot 2: Sculpture*, the second annual exhibition in October 1969, ensuring that it was a more professional affair than its predecessor.[28] For the young dealer it presented at once an idealistic and a practical proposition by offering a ready-formed group of artists – without the normal restrictions on what a commercial gallery could show – and without the necessity of renting a gallery space.[29]

New Sculpture 1969, first shown in Stevenage town centre, comprised large-scale, newly commissioned sculptures by Brener, Evison, Fagin, Hemsworth, Hide and Louw. It was one of many similar initiatives by the Arts Council and others that took place in the late 1960s and early 1970s, which attempted to funnel the ever-increasing numbers of sculptures being produced by graduates of British art schools back into the public realm. This was despite the fact that the growth of invention in sculpture depended precisely upon its refusal to compromise with the demands exhibiting in this realm made. At some level the public may have intuited this contradiction and the exhibition was beset by vandalism.[30] In collapsing studio and exhibition space together, the Depot approached the problem from a different direction. Hide saw the advantages of working at Stockwell in a quite straightforward manner: it allowed him to make and show sculptures at a size he could not have done otherwise. Beyond this, he thought that the group 'generates a critical and competitive atmosphere' and was 'more meaningful and effective in terms of communication than exhibiting in isolation'.[31]

In contrast Brener saw a much less neutral relationship between the Depot and the sculpture that was made for it. As he saw it, it was imperative that the work made there acknowledge the conditions under which it was produced: 'Freedom exists when one recognises the nature of the pressures and one's own response to them.'[32] In 1970 Brener was invited to select the follow-up exhibition to *New Sculpture 1969*. He chose six young artists, and asked them to make sculptures that directly responded to the open-air sites that the exhibition toured to. The exhibition, and Brener's selection of artists and artworks, continued his attack on a permanent or 'hermetic' sculpture. Attempting a resolution outside of the special case of the Depot, the exhibition also specifically criticised its predecessor and the many similar exhibitions of these years, expressing 'a disenchantment with the usual formula of taking self-contained sculptures and placing them in situations to which they bear no relevance.' Brener hoped that a 'free temporary intervention… by artists is a healthy step towards the dialogue essential between artist and public', although this exhibition too suffered from vandalism.[33]

By the time of *Stockwell Depot 2: Sculpture*, difficulties had arisen within the group. 'Attitudes and ambitions seem to have shifted even since [the first annual exhibition] last summer… there is a general feeling among them… that this could be the last time they exhibit together in the building… In trying not to influence or be influenced by one another their relationships are aggressive, competitive, and strongly critical.'[34] One critic, in an observation that could well apply to later generations of artists at Stockwell, suggested that this abrasiveness was not just internal: 'in their relations with the outer world… they are rough-spoken, suspicious and "uncompromising"'.[35] Over the course of a Scandinavian tour of sculpture from Stockwell, which was organised by Nigel Greenwood and the British Council, the differences in ideology became unavoidable.

During 1970, Barkley, Dunlop, Fagin, Fowler, Hemsworth

26 Brener's work was considered too large for inclusion in *Survey 68: Abstract Sculpture*. Amongst the other artists included were four sculptors (Tony Shafrazi, John Panting, Stephen Furlonger, Adrian Phipps-Hunt) who worked in converted warehouses in Tabernacle Street, east London, suggesting the advantages of spaces where dealers or bureaucrats could easily visit a number of artists in an afternoon.

27 Barkley, Brener, Evison, Fagin, Hemsworth, Hide and Louw, *Studio International*, *op.cit.*

28 Greenwood had met Louw at the first Depot exhibition, an event he later remembered as 'rather chaotic… you couldn't find anyone, you couldn't find the way in'. Nigel Greenwood, Artists' Lives interview, British Library.

29 'We lived with this wonderful vision that things could only get better, of progress, and with that the belief that the public, the paying public, would come', Catherine Moseley (ed), 'Interview with Nigel Greenwood', *Conception: Conceptual Documents 1968–1972*, exhibition catalogue, Norwich Gallery, Norwich, 2001.

30 After vandalism at Stevenage, plans to tour the exhibition to Bristol, Harrogate and Billingham were abandoned and it was subsequently shown in more restricted conditions in Wollaston, in the grounds of a factory, and at Newcastle Civic Centre, Newcastle.

31 Barkley, Brener, Evison, Fagin, Hemsworth, Hide and Louw, *Studio International*, *op.cit.*, p.36.

32 Roland Brener, 'Concerns of Emerging Sculptors', *Studio International*, *ibid.*, p.25; see p.162 in present volume.

33 *New Sculpture 1970* was shown at Basildon Town Square in Essex; at the University of Kent, Canterbury; and in parks in Birmingham and Norwich. Exhibiting artists were Roger Bates, Elona Bennett, Glyn Foulkes, Carl Plackman and Tim Head, all of whom were students or recent graduates.

34 Anne Seymour, introduction to *Stockwell Depot 2: Sculpture*, exhibition pamphlet, Stockwell Depot, London, 1969, n.p.

35 John Russell, *ARTnews*, November 1969, p.46.

and Louw all left the Depot.[36] By then a mutual and what was to prove long-lasting antipathy had developed between Hide and Evison, and by the beginning of 1971 the Depot was administered in two halves. Evison was the chief tenant in The Annexe, having taken on the series of small rooms originally leased by Hemsworth; Hide was in charge of the rest, and had officially taken on the spaces that had previously been used rent-free. Evison kept a space in the Depot until the end of its existence, and participated in one of the subsequent annual exhibitions, but the Depot of the 1970s, and the public position it staked out, was driven by Hide.

For about a year from the summer of 1968 the painter Gary Wragg had a space in The Annexe. Fairly soon after he had left this was taken over by the Scottish painter John McLean. Like Wragg and in common to many British painters at the time, McLean developed a hard-edged style in response to the American 'post-painterly abstraction', that had grown in the wake of Abstract Expressionism; this style was often known as 'Greenbergian' after its chief promoter.[37] McLean thought the paintings of American abstract artists Kenneth Noland and Morris Louis 'seemed to open up the future', but that it was only after loosening up his approach that he felt able to work with their 'directness and scale.'[38] A move away from the cool detachment of the 1960s, and towards more painterly improvised applications and open, broken colour was common to many of the painters at Stockwell – although not necessarily with an Abstract Expressionist intensity of feeling. For McLean, the space available to him at the Depot aided this transition.

In 1971 McLean exhibited paintings made at Stockwell in a summer show at the Serpentine Gallery, newly opened in a former tea pavilion in Hyde Park, London. Run by the Arts Council, and subject to some criticism for its focus on painting and sculpture over other diverse media, which proliferated during this time, the Serpentine became an important venue for Stockwell artists.

Following McLean into the Depot, and occupying the adjacent studio to him, was John Golding. A painter and distinguished historian of modern art, best known for his work on Cubism, Golding had taught McLean at the Courtauld Institute of Art, London. He remembered his studio as 'a beautiful space but also squalid'. At least a decade older than the other artists at the Depot, Golding was something of an odd man out, detached from the boisterous drinking culture – centred around the local Marquis of Lorne pub on the corner of Combermere Road – that had developed after the first group broke up. Few of the other artists recall seeing him at the Depot. Although sharing an attraction to large-scale painting, Golding's response to postwar American painting remained rooted in the more cerebral attitudes of earlier abstraction. He did not participate in any of the annual exhibitions, and left the Depot sometime in the mid-1970s. Eddy Hemsley, a student of Peter Hide's at Norwich School of Art, Norwich, arrived during 1969 to work as his assistant and continued to occupy space at the Depot until 1975. At around the same time Alan Bucket began work as an assistant to Evison, being paid with free studio space in The Annexe. Hemsley moved between studios in Hide's and Evison's sections, although he remembered associating most closely with Evison and McLean, who encouraged him to take up painting in addition to sculpture. Hemsley was popular with many at the Depot, although he was not included in any of the annual exhibitions. After a move to New York – where he briefly worked for Louw – Hemsley stopped working as an artist.[39]

During 1970 Brener, Hemsworth and Golding all exhibited at Greenwood's new space, Nigel Greenwood Inc Ltd in Chelsea, London. Brener showed a version of his *Deep Space Installation* (1970; p.67), which had debuted in Scandinavia. Fully adaptable to the proportions of the room in which it was shown, in it he seems to step over the line between sculpture and installation. In the same year, Evison had the first of two solo exhibitions with Kasmin in New Bond Street, London. Since Prospect 68 in Dusseldorf two years earlier, the dealer had supported

36 Fagin began working on community art and Fowler on commercial projects. For much of the 1970s Hemsworth produced text-based conceptual art, before switching to a kind of post-Pop painting at the beginning of the 1980s. Andrew Dunlop moved to Derby on a more fulltime basis; Barkley also went north, teaching at Hull College of Art, before returning to Canada, where he taught and continued to make modernist abstract sculpture. Louw shifted further away from his New Generation roots into the international avant garde; he gained some success and moved to New York in the early 1970s.

37 *Post-Painterly Abstraction* was the title of a 1964 exhibition Greenberg curated at the Los Angeles County Museum of Art, Los Angeles.

38 'The Declaration of Arbroath: Bill Hare Interviews John McLean', *Alba*, no.6, winter 1987, p.11.

39 There are many anecdotes which reveal how some viewed the Depot's atmosphere: tales of rats running along studio walls, holding one paw up to shield their eyes from stray welding sparks; and comparisons to Joseph Conrad's 1899 novella *Heart of Darkness*. For his part, Hemsley came to believe the Depot was haunted. Less phantasmically, he once accompanied the art collector Lord Guinness to the Marquis of Lorne – afterwards the landlord insisted the head of the famous brewing family must have been an imposter.

him through helping with the purchase of materials and equipment, therefore allowing him to devote more time to his sculpture. Evison's three sculptures, all of which sold, were more stylistically coherent than those he had shown in the Depot exhibitions. They married his previous inventiveness with a new sophistication, producing 'an elegantly disciplined casualness'[40] that now seems to look forward to the rest of his career as a sculptor. The proportions of the architectural sculpture of Caro or Tucker (as literalised by Brener) followed the proportions of an everyday, box-like room. In contrast, the uprightness of Evison's sculptures at Kasmin's suggested a building or monument seen externally, even as their structures were opened up.

During the early 1970s, Kasmin sold Evison's sculptures to businessman and art collector Alistair McAlpine, the only serious British collector of the New Generation, and to the Boston collector Louis Cabot – a purchase that led to Evison's inclusion in the group exhibition *Six British Sculptors* (1972) at the city's Museum of Fine Arts.[41] Nothing, however, sold from Evison's second exhibition with Kasmin at the beginning of that year, where he exhibited lively open sculptures in which curved steel contrasted with wooden planks, salvaged from the Depot. This says little about the relative quality of the work in the two exhibitions, and much more about a slowing down of the art market and a shift away from the taste for modernist abstraction in Britain. Having been the most important contemporary commercial venue in London through much of the 1960s, Kasmin closed his gallery – the archetypal white cube – less than 12 months after Evison's second exhibition there. Attenuated commercial opportunities and a growing apathy, even hostility, towards modernist sculpture – particularly that associated with St Martin's – would form the backdrop to the activity at the Depot through the 1970s. In the summer of 1970 Brener, Evison, Hemsworth and Louw exhibited in *British Sculpture Out of the Sixties* at the ICA. One critic used the exhibition to suggest: 'Really, British sculpture of the sixties never existed. It was a publicity kick that sold a lot of large objects to American collectors.'[42]

The third Depot exhibition, *Stockwell Depot: Peter Hide, Roland Brener: An Independent Exhibition* (1970), opened towards the end of the ICA exhibition's run. The variety of the first two exhibitions was replaced by the visually complementary, yet clearly distinct contributions of Brener and Hide, which spread from the roof through to the Upper Pillar Room. In an introductory statement they distanced themselves from the previous group. Brener's temporary installations of fishing twine and UV light were only fully thought through just prior to being made. The exhibition asserted Hide's independence from the New Generation and Caro in particular, although a trace of 1960s colour remained in some sculptures. His austere tri-and quadpods developed in more concentrated fashion the structural literalist tension found in Brener's sculpture. Hide stated that his 'approach to sculpture is essentially corporeal. I allow myself to be conditioned by the demands of the physical world... an element's presence is dictated by mechanical necessity rather than visual preference.'[43] The exhibition was well received, though critic Edward Lucie-Smith sounded a wry note, observing that the pair:

> denounce the various art bureaucracies in a catalogue statement. Good luck to them. One cannot help noting, however, that this is precisely the kind of art which must in the end have dealings with the people whom the artists concerned most despise... In art, irony need not be conscious.[44]

A period of change: Stockwell in flux

In the autumn of 1970, Brener moved to the United States to teach at University of California in Santa Barbara. He returned to the Depot the following year and was due to participate in the 1972 Depot exhibition when an offer to teach at the University of Iowa, Iowa City came up and he left Britain for good, eventually settling in Canada. During the winter of 1970–71, artists Gilbert & George – St Martin's graduates with a very different outlook to that which generally pervaded the Depot – made a series of large paintings in the room next to the Loggia, for an exhibition at Whitechapel Art Gallery.[45] Over the course of 1971, Rita

40 Anne Seymour, 'London Commentary', *Studio International*, vol.179, no.921, April 1970, p.184.

41 Alistair McAlpine built studios for Phillip King and Tim Scott and helped with the construction of the Greenwich Studios. He bought sculpture from Smart and Evison (the latter on behalf of the Whitworth Art Gallery, Manchester) and helped Hemsley purchase steel for his sculptures.

42 Paul Overy, 'British Sculptors and American Reviewers', *Financial Times*, 21 August 1970.

43 Brener and Hide, *Studio International*, *op.cit.*

44 Edward Lucie-Smith, 'Force of Tradition', *The Observer*, 20 September 1970.

45 In 2010, Gilbert & George's six large triptychs *The Paintings (with Us in the Nature)* (1971) were sold to the Kröller-Müller Museum, Otterlo for over 2.5 million euros, ensuring that these were, by a considerable margin, the most expensive works of art produced at Stockwell.

Marshall left her studio in The Annexe, while Richard (Dick) James (a painter) and John Foster (a sculptor) took up studios in Hide's half of the Depot. The group who had departed over 1970 had left a large amount of debris behind, and Hide, assisted by Hemsley and Geoff Hollow, a friend of Foster's and a self-taught painter who would later take up a studio in the Depot, spent a substantial part of the year clearing up. James took over Brener's space in the Upper Pillar Room. Foster, only 20 years old when he arrived in the Depot, set up in the Loggia and began working for Hide as an assistant.

In 1972 Jennifer Durrant arrived, initially subletting part of the Upper Pillar Room from James; after his departure a couple of years later, she took over the whole of the space, where she remained under 1979. Durrant had already begun to establish her career, and during her first years at Stockwell work by her was purchased by the Arts Council Collection. She visited New York in 1972 with Evison, who had travelled from London with Gouk, a painter involved with the sculpture department at St Martin's and who would play an important role in the Depot from the mid-1970s; McLean was also in the city at the time. In New York, Durrant was introduced to Greenberg and to the expanses of recent American painting. Exhibitions were supplemented with visits to the studios of painters Kenneth Noland, Jules Olitski and Larry Poons. As Durrant later remembered, 'I saw these huge pictures for the first time, without reading or understanding historically about the position that they held... But I know that I identified, absolutely, with what I came into contact with.'[46] A day trip to see the studio of American abstract sculptor David Smith, which was preserved at Bolton Landing in New York State, had a lasting effect on Evison. He and Durrant also visited Evison's collector, Louis Cabot, in Boston and the studios of sculptors Willard Boepple, Joel Perlman, James Wolfe and the New Generation sculptor Isaac Witkin in Bennington, Vermont.

James attended the Slade School of Fine Art in the early 1960s, though did not show much in the latter half of the decade; the paintings he exhibited at Durham Arts Centre, Durham in the summer prior to his 1972 Depot debut broke a 'period of self-imposed isolation'.[47] His handling of the scale favoured by Depot painters involved dramatic swirls or sashes of thick impasto colour – 'yellow, lilac, turquoise, orange, green' – or monochrome backgrounds interrupted by collaged scraps of crumpled canvas, salvaged from failed paintings.[48] Sales seem to have been a problem: the same three private collectors are listed on both the 1972 and 1973 exhibition pamphlets and there are no paintings by him in British public collections. Large size, copious paint consumption, and the fact he would 'work out of surplus, throwing a lot away' meant James's material costs were high. Over 1971–72 he spent more on paint, canvas and stretchers than the £360 his studio cost, while to produce the six large (3.6 × 1.8 metres) and three small paintings he made for the 1973 Depot exhibition, *Stockwell Depot: Peter Hide, Sculpture; Richard James, Paintings*, cost £332, with £200 spent on paint alone. James showed in the Serpentine Gallery exhibition *Serpentine Painting 73* (1973), and after he left the Depot was included in surveys of British painting mounted by the Hayward Gallery and the Royal Academy of Arts, London.

The Depot exhibition in 1971 was a solo show of works by Hide that reinstated his structural literalist sculpture of previous years but with a new toughness and bulk. Caroline Tisdall favourably compared his sculptures to recent work by Caro.[49] Painter Frank Bowling remembered that through the 1970s Hide was widely seen at St Martin's as mounting a serious challenge to Caro, 'because of his art, and because of his personality'. It seems likely that this idea, which may well have been helped because of the situation he was creating at Stockwell, originated at around this moment. The Depot exhibitions of 1972 and 1973 showed sculpture by Hide alongside paintings by James. Some of the sculptures Hide showed at the Depot were named to emphasise their extent: *36 Foot Span* (1971; p.76) or *48 Foot Wave* (1971). Outside of the Depot his *Arch* (1971; p.75), erected in South Africa in 1971, was 25 metres long; *Big Ring* (1970) – twice unsuccessfully erected, first at the Royal Park, Oslo in 1970 and then at Marble Hill House, Twickenham in 1973 – was 36.5 metres in diameter. There were large public commissions in Durham and Southampton; *Compression Pillar* (1972; p.83) was sited in the latter city as part of Peter Stuyvesant's *City Sculpture Project* of 1972. Brener reduced his material to a minimum in order to make his sculptures 'integral' with the space they were shown in; Hide seems to have wanted to justify his sculptures' presence through

46 Jennifer Durrant, interview with the author, January 2015.
47 *Richard James*, exhibition pamphlet, Durham Arts Centre, Durham, 1972.
48 Mary Whistler, 'Richard James: Consort Gallery', *Arts Review*, vol.27, no.3, 7 February 1975, p.72.
49 The exhibition was titled *Stockwell Depot: Peter Hide: An Independent Exhibition* (1971). Caroline Tisdall, *The Guardian*, October, 1971.

Roland Brener and Peter Hide on the roof at Stockwell Depot, London, 1970
with Peter Hide, *Tower* (1969–70)

Gilbert & George's temporary studio at Stockwell Depot, London, 1971
with *The Paintings (with Us in the Nature)* (1971)

the severe presentation of sheer physical fact. A more internal justification came from his structural literalism, which tended to push or compress his sculptures together, where Brener's had implied the possibility of a springing outward. Hide viewed his austere, sometimes bluntly massive sculptures as monuments to rationalism or logic.

In the summer of 1973 Hide and Foster exhibited at Marble Hill House. The exhibition comprised a retrospective of the sculpture Hide had made since 1966, but was Foster's first public showing. For Fenella Crichton in *Art International* magazine, Hide's desire to see his sculptures in a landscape setting had become 'an astoundingly effective reality'; his *Trapezium* (1973; p.87) presented 'huge curved shafts [which] define a shape of exultant purity, achieving a perfect interaction with the surrounding landscape, as the beauty of each is sharpened by the other'. Crichton thought Foster's 'constructions bristle with an aggressive energy... [like] a menacing assembly of war-machines.'[50] Intimations of aggressiveness, ugliness or violence would become a feature of reviews of Stockwell Sculpture through the 1970s. Seeming to continue the early reviewers' response to the brewery building itself, this stance perhaps prevented a more objective response to the sculpture, though may have reflected the demeanour of the sculptors, who, as one commentator later put it 'were not adverse to cultivating an aggressive image'.[51] By the time of the Marble Hill exhibition, Hide was beginning to grow tired of his structural literalist sculpture, feeling its 'aridity' was limiting and that the distinction it made between his and Caro's sculpture was a form of 'concocted originality'.

Beginnings of Stockwell Sculpture

During 1973, St Martin's Advanced Course students Katherine Gili and Anthony Smart joined Foster and Hide at the Depot. The work of the four would define Stockwell Sculpture through the 1970s. When she had first moved to London, Gili had a SPACE studio at St Katharine Docks. On taking up a studio in south London, she was excited by the larger space at her disposal at Stockwell, the commitment to sculpture of those around her, and was more or less oblivious to the icy draughts and the water which constantly ran down the walls. Smart's journey to St Martin's was bound up with Stockwell. At Hull College of Art he was taught by Alan Barkley and had been impressed by reproductions of Hide's sculpture in *Studio International*: he later called Hide's *Compression Piece* (1971) 'a zero point in sculpture'. Visiting St Martin's, Smart was disappointed by what he saw as the lack of sculpture being made in the department, and was only persuaded to apply because of his familiarity with Stockwell.[52] None of the quartet kept a full-time studio through to the end of the decade, which suggests some of the problems associated with working in such a close and competitive atmosphere were evident. Yet even when away from the Depot they worked to the rhythm of the annual exhibitions, and in a spirit of competition, as much as one of emulation, took on a communal identity to a larger degree than the Depot sculptors who preceded them.

Following in the Depot's footsteps and prompted by SPACE's success, there was a large expansion in the conversion of disused premises into studios funded by the Arts Council. By 1976 SPACE controlled 17 properties with 232 artists. Acme Studios, founded in 1972, originally concentrated on converting derelict houses into accommodation or individual studios for artists, later turning to larger warehouse conversions. Alongside these 'models of collaborative self-help'[53] were a large number of independent studios. Most were single properties, however the individually occupied warehouses in Butler's Wharf on the south bank of the Thames would eventually spread over 18,000 square metres of studio space. Other notable schemes in south London included Dilston Grove in Southwark and the Greenwich Studios, for which Smart would leave Stockwell to help develop in 1974. Gili later took over his space at Greenwich when he moved to Yorkshire in 1978; and Foster left the Depot in 1975 to renovate a farm in rural Norfolk. Like the Depot, Greenwich Studios were closely associated with St Martin's and had an emphasis on modernist abstraction.[54] In 1976 *Artscribe* magazine was founded,

50 Fenella Crichton, 'London Letter', *Art International*, vol.17, no.8, October 1973, p.39.

51 Veronica Sekules, introduction to *Hardingham Sculpture Workshop: Selection of Sculpture*, exhibition catalogue, Sainsbury Centre for Visual Art, University of East Anglia, Norwich, 1986, p.5.

52 Anthony Smart, interviews with the author, 2010 and 2014. Elona Bennett, included in Brener's *New Sculpture 1970*, was also drawn to St Martin's by her experience of visiting Stockwell. Shirley Cameron, *St Martin's Sculpture Department in the 60s and After: An Investigation*, unpublished, p.52.

53 See Kit Wedd, Lucy Peltz and Cathy Ross, *Creative Quarters: the Art World in London 1700–2000*, Museum of London, London, 2001, pp.146–49.

partly in response to the lack of discussion on the large amount of activity taking place in London studios: it contained much of the best writing about the Depot.

The artists of the 1970s – including the sculptors and painters at the Depot – were more frequently from ordinary backgrounds than those of the 1960s, borne along by the growth in art-school education that had taken place through that decade. Whereas some of the New Generation had studied at Oxford or Cambridge, many of the abstract sculptors at St Martin's in the early 1970s came from provincial art schools.[55] The New Generation were more likely to have access to family money in addition to the stipends and sales of the buoyant art market of the 1960s; but for the artists that followed them, private sales were rare, and were only very occasionally supplemented by purchases by public collections.[56] Hide had some private means but the others could only sustain their practice through the combination of the cheap space available at Stockwell and the part-time teaching art schools provided. It was common for artists, living frugally, to get by with two days' teaching a week, allowing the rest of the time to devote to their own art. Arts Council grants provided occasional supplements.

The groundwork for the Stockwell group's rethinking of the legacy of the New Generation was partly laid by two changes at St Martin's. In 1970 Alan Gouk was put in charge of the Advanced Course and in 1971 the Diploma in Art and Design (DipAD) split in two. William Tucker organised a 'B' course with a focus on object-based modernist abstract sculpture, and Peter Kardia ran a conceptually orientated 'A' course.[57] The split was an attempt to accommodate a seemingly unbridgeable gulf in understanding of what sculpture was and consequently what sculptural pedagogy could consist of; that is, between an attitude rooted in the New Generation's investigation of the modernist object and an approach which denied that sculpture needed to be a physical object, so that – as Tucker complained – 'Sculpture has been used deliberately and perversely to describe natural phenomena, dramatic events, photographs and so forth.'[58] Gouk had run the 'rough and tumble' of the St Martin's Forums – expanded semi-public crits, where sculpture and occasionally painting was set up and often harshly criticised – since 1967. His appointment ensured that the Advanced Course would continue its focus on the mainstream as established by the New Generation. A large number of students arrived sympathetic to Tucker's and Gouk's ideas; Gili remembered that sculpture 'was all we talked about'.[59]

Hide thought William Tucker 'set the intellectual agenda of the seventies'.[60] His teaching at St Martin's – where Hide, Smart, Gili and Evison all returned – was supplemented by his writing, of which his book on early modern sculpture, *The Language of Sculpture* (1974), was particularly important: Auguste Rodin and Edgar Degas would become important to Gili, Smart, Foster and Hide, as would the broader history of sculpture. In the 1960s Tucker saw abstract sculpture's precedents in 'painting and poetry'; his writing of the following decade attempted to establish a sculptural basis for sculpture.[61] An especially clear summation of his ideas came in his introduction to the 1975 survey exhibition *The Condition of Sculpture* at the Hayward Gallery, London. As an alternative to the myriad objects and activities which were then being claimed as sculpture, Tucker proposed sculpture was a physically limited object, in the world, but distinct from it. He envisioned a 'freestanding' sculpture: '"Free", as wholly exposed to our perception, in light; "standing", as withstanding the pull of the earth.' At its core, freestanding sculpture was explicitly a rejection of 'pictorialism' (which removed things from the world and made sculpture a 'hollow and perverse surrogate-painting').[62] Tucker shared the preference of the early Stockwell artists for the physical over the visual,

54 See Alice Correla, David Waterworth and David Webb, *Uncaught Hares: Painting and Sculpture at Greenwich Studios 1974–1994*, The Stephen Lawrence Gallery, London, 2012.

55 Robert Persey in conversation with the author, November 2014. Anthony Caro and Phillip King studied at Cambridge; William Tucker studied at Oxford.

56 Hide and Louw sold sculptures to the Tate collection in 1970, with later purchases in 1988 and 2013 respectively. Brener was due to sell a sculpture to the Tate, possibly his *Deep Space Installation*. He sent it to the Tate unassembled in a box without instructions, which he then refused to supply – the sale did not go through. Hide's *Glass Tower* (1970) and *Beryl* (1975); Evison's *Black Heat* (1972) and *Number Seven* (1975); and Gili's *Vertical III* (1975) and *Pistil* (1979) were all sold to the Arts Council Collection. Smart sold one work, *Tamarind X* (1977).

57 The 'A' and 'B' courses at St Martin's were established in 1971 when the sculpture half of the DipAD was split in two. The 'B' course was for most – though not all – of the period closest to the Advanced Course in its approach.

58 William Tucker, 'What Sculpture Is, Part 1', *Studio International*, vol.188, no.972, December 1974, p.234.

59 Katherine Gili in conversation with the author, November 2014. Charles Hewlings, on the Advanced Course in 1972–73, remembered 'raging encounters between people of very different temperaments and with very different points of view; from outside the institution of course, it would all look more or less similar, but from inside all these voices were very individual and distinct and often at complete loggerheads.' Hester Westley, *Rites of Passage: Tradition and Transmission at St Martin's School of Art, 1960–1980*, PhD, Courtauld Institute of Art, London, 2007, p.204.

60 Peter Hide in conversation with the author, October 2014.

61 William Tucker, 'Questionnaire', *First*, St Martin's School of Art, London, 1962, n.p.

62 William Tucker, introduction to *The Condition of Sculpture*, exhibition catalogue, Hayward Gallery, London, 1975, pp.6–9.

but rejected their environmental stance. Also, and importantly for the work that would develop at the Depot, freestanding sculpture rejected the need for the adjustment to circumstance – which was so important to Brener – reinstating the modernist ideal in which the problem of sculpture's placelessness could be overcome through attention to its internal physical properties. In Tucker's teaching, and in the sculpture at the Depot, the 'idea of the end of modern sculpture' was met by a strong reinstatement of first principles.

A new break with the New Generation

In 1974, *Stockwell Depot: New Sculpture*, the seventh annual, showed Gili, Smart, Foster and Hide together; the following year the quartet were joined by Evison, on what was to be the last of the annual exhibitions he participated in, as well as five painters, most of whom were not from the Depot. Across these two years Gili, Smart, Foster and Hide – the first three still in their mid-twenties – began to find their feet in a new way of working. Their almost exclusive focus was upon steel, generally in its raw state. This was common to many sculptors at the time. Caro stopped using applied colour, or restricted it to blacks or browns, almost as soon as the decade began; as did New Generation sculptors Phillip King and Tim Scott, who both also turned away from the plastics that had been central to their work. Scott began forging and his more-involved manipulation of steel, and his own journey back into the history of sculpture, would be important to Stockwell Sculpture. Hide and Foster were drawn to the sculpture of American abstract artist Michael Steiner, which they saw on a trip to New York shortly after the Marble Hill exhibition. Steiner 'showed how to compress cubist elements into powerful masses suggestive of weight by using thickness expressively'.[63] In amongst this wider use of steel, the Stockwell artists' dedication to it was perhaps at the root of the accusations of dogmatism that gathered around them.

Though their reaction was very different to that which had characterised the first two years of activity at the Depot, the image of 1960s sculpture remained with them as a powerful negative, something they did *not* want to be. In line with Tucker, they wanted to establish a sculptural basis for sculpture, and set themselves in opposition to pictorialism, particularly in the form of Caro's open spreading of discrete elements through space. There was a growing feeling that too much had been lost in the gains constructed sculpture had made under the New Generation, particularly that the flat planes derived from Cubism, which formed the constituent elements of Caro's sculpture, effected too harsh a removal from the give and take of space. There was a particular distaste for what was seen as the overly casual way that Caro's 'magic glue' could join his parts together; structural literalism's emphasis on a physical rather visual structure was an important beginning. They attempted a more concentrated sculpture: on the one hand this expressed itself through emphatically built, closely integrated construction that gradually developed into an active manipulation of steel on the other it led to denser, more volumetric structures, that attempted to reconcile the freedom of constructed steel sculpture with the physicality of pre-modern sculpture.

The expressive content of New Generation sculpture was based in the unreal or the unworldly: whether as a quasi-surrealistic incongruity, or as a miraculous opening outward. The development of Stockwell Sculpture was also the development of a general expressive content: something that Foster and Hide were perhaps most conscious of, with Smart more resolutely formalist – at least in his way of talking. This content – which they would each establish their own relationship with – had its origins in their understanding of material. Where New Generation sculpture used steel in ways that denied its weight, Stockwell Sculpture emphasised steel as a material both resistant and ductile, one whose full structural potential could only be achieved with difficulty, with a slow movement towards resolution. It was correspondingly restrained, tending to hold itself together, to be inward facing even as it established itself as blunt physical presence. The sculpture they made over 1974 and 1975 was rigidly angular. Among the more striking sculptures from these years are Smart's structural literalist works from the 1974 exhibition, or, similarly concerned with enclosed volume, Hide's monumental early masterpiece *Pomeroy* (1974–75; p.117), which was shown at the *The Condition of Sculpture* exhibition. More open were Foster's stiffly pirouetting *Three Cornered* (1975; p.108) from the 1975 exhibition, or the group Gili showed in 1974, which Gouk later distinguished from Caro as being 'genuinely constructed rather than assembled'.[64]

Evison was not involved in the close interaction that took

63 Peter Hide, letter to the author, 2008.

place between the other four, nor did he seem to suffer their anxiety of influence, which was felt most keenly by Hide. He later wrote that 'new and original art after 1970 does not declare itself as self-evidently new and original... Today's best art has a subtle newness and appears similar to the art of the immediate past.'[65] Where the other Stockwell sculptors were beginning to work in tougher, more spartan fashion, since his 1972 exhibition at Kasmin Limited, Evison had continued to refine an improvised, elegant and open abstract sculpture. One branch of his endeavour was rectilinear, with bland lengths of steel assembled with a throwaway meticulousness. The other, including the three works exhibited at the Depot in 1975, involved a contrast between aluminium and steel, and between limb-like struts, and space-cupping curves. These works took off from the optimistic freedom of Caro's or Scott's sculpture of the late 1960s: 'sheets of supple steel dip and swoop, sometimes slipping under one another with sinuous dexterity and sometimes reaching into space and forming arcs of graceful precision.'[66] Since 1972 Evison had shown outside of the Depot at group exhibitions in Holland Park and Berkshire (with Hide and Foster also in the latter) and was included in a touring exhibition of painting and sculpture selected for purchase for the Arts Council by Lord Dufferin, who was Kasmin's former business partner. In the spring of 1975 he was shown in Germany, as part of a presentation of contemporary British art organised by the Serpentine Gallery. His *Sculpture IV* (1975; p.105) was purchased by the Whitworth Art Gallery in Manchester with the funds provided by McAlpine.

The Depot exhibition of 1975, *Stockwell Depot: Studio Exhibition; New Painting and Sculpture*, overlapped with Tucker's *The Condition of Sculpture*, in which Hide, Smart, Gili and Evison showed, and an outdoor sculpture exhibition at Greenwich Studios, which included all five of the sculptors at Stockwell. There must have been a sense of possibilities opening up – at least for Smart and Gili. Yet the exhibitions acted as a lightening rod for critics weary of St Martin's sculpture. Peter Fuller thought that the artworks in *The Condition of Sculpture* evidenced 'tedious formal preoccupations that have little relevance outside a limited sector of the contemporary art world'.[67] Richard Cork called it a 'tightly unified sculptural club'.[68] Lawrence Alloway, noting Caro's absence, suggested that nonetheless he was the originator of Tucker's ideas and that many of the sculptures on display were direct glosses of Caro's work.[69] Art critic and curator Edward Sharp surveyed all three shows: 'the Greenwich and Stockwell heavy metal divisions mobilised south of the river... [an] alliance of tired predators... the centrifugal force of mainstream metal sculpture.'[70]

In the spirit of these reviews, one critic thought the inclusion of painters in the 1975 exhibition, 'a wise decision from the point of view of those who are sick from being fed on an exclusive diet of formalisms perpetuated by the St Martin's ethos'.[71] The paintings were chosen by an informal committee of non-Depot artists comprising Alan Gouk, Geoff Rigden and Fred Pollock. The trio asked Stephenie Bergman to show alongside them. Bergman knew Hide from her time at St Martin's and was then working more as a collagist than a painter, stitching panels of canvas into abstract designs.[72] John McLean was the fifth in the line-up, and the only painter included with a studio at the Depot. The painting at Stockwell was formed by looking to the common territory of 'post-painterly abstraction': Jack Bush, Helen Frankenthaler, Morris Louis, Kenneth Noland and Jules Olitski, supplemented by some of the more 'colour field' Abstract Expressionists, Adolph Gottlieb, Jackson Pollock and Clyfford Still (*not* Willem de Kooning); as the 1970s progressed Hans Hofmann's work grew in significance. Of course not all the Stockwell artists responded in the same way to these artists. Their paintings were filtered through individual sensibilities, along with a myriad other influences: McLean and Pollock were more resolutely abstract, the former tending towards delicacy, the latter a robust breadth. Rigden's closely woven marks were placed with a sensibility somewhere between directness and irony. Gouk's paintings were turbulently and insistently physical, sombre in tone. 'Greenbergian' is the beginning of a description of these paintings rather than, as often seems to be the case,

64 Alan Gouk, 'Steel Sculpture Part II: From Scott, Tucker and Panting to Present', *abstract critical*, 30 May 2014, http://abstractcritical.com/article/steel-sculpture-part-ii-from-scott-tucker-and-panting-to-the-present, accessed 15 June 2014.

65 David Evison, 'Early Encounters with Caro' in Sam Cornish (ed), *Collaborating With Caro*, University of the Arts, London, 2014, p.16.

66 Fenella Crichton, 'London', *Art International*, September 1975, p.54.

67 Peter Fuller, 'The Condition of Sculpture', *Connoisseur*, vol.189, no.762, August 1975, p.327.

68 Richard Cork, 'A Narrow Vision of Sculpture' (1975), *Everything Seemed Possible: Art in the 1970s*, Yale University Press, New Haven, CT and London, 2003.

69 Lawrence Alloway, 'Caro's Art – Tucker's Choice', *Artforum*, October 1975, pp.65–71.

70 Edward Sharp, 'Metal Manners', *Artscribe*, no.1, January/February, 1976.

71 Crichton, 'London', *Art International*, *op.cit.*

72 Fred Pollock and Stephenie Bergman had exhibited the previous year at Garage Art Ltd., a short-lived enterprise of Kasmin's. The gallery had the disused feel of a warehouse, reflecting what was fast becoming fashionable.

the final word on the matter. It is also worth emphasising that although some were well versed in Greenberg's writings, this was not always necessarily the case.[73] And even for those who closely followed American criticism, their engagement was always, as Durrant's had been on the 1972 trip, first and foremost visual. Gouk saw the 'vast expanse of pinkish cream palette knifings, with subtle colour transitions' of a Clyfford Still at the Tate Gallery in 1964; at around the same time that Rigden saw his first Hofmann at Waddington Gallery, London, 'through the window, burning off the back wall'.[74]

The dim light in most of its spaces meant the Depot was not an amenable place to show paintings, but they would continue to be a feature of the annual exhibitions. They were given space by increasingly compacted sculptures: an allowance that Brener's or Louw's desire to create 'situations' had actively discouraged. There also is a certain logic in showing paintings alongside sculptures that were attempting to rid themselves of pictorial qualities: a securing of each discipline's 'area of competence' by mutual reinforcement as much as internal self-criticism.[75] More pertinently, the painters and sculptors were united in making art ultimately concerned with feeling – though their means were formal, their ends were expressive. There was a broad, and more or less unquestioned, consensus on what an art object was, in what way it was to be responded to. The number of painters from outside the Depot meant the exhibitions were not just displays 'of the St Martin's ethos', but a united front for modernist abstraction.

Proscriptions, intransigence, defensiveness and defiance

Hide and Evison were shown together at the Serpentine Gallery's *Summer Show 2* in 1976. Evison had moved away from the contrasting materials and curves that had defined his sculpture, towards angular, box-like structures. A similar body of work was shown in a solo exhibition at the Museum of Modern Art, Oxford that autumn. McLean approved of the restriction, suggesting it allowed the space within Evison's sculpture ('given parity with the stuff of the work') to become 'more tangible' and offering 'all the rich rewards of classic restraint'.[76] The exhibition was the high point of Hide's career in Britain – he showed 11 sculptures and Caro purchased his *Sidestep* (1976) from the exhibition. Hide and Evison's exhibition was part of a run of art associated with the Depot to be displayed at the Serpentine. Among the sculptors, in 1977 Gili took part in the summer exhibition, followed by Foster in 1979, along with Kim Earley, who showed in the Depot that year. Gili and Durrant were also included in the Arts Council's *Hayward Annual 1979*.[77] Despite these votes of approval from officialdom, Evison registered a lack of interest in his and Hide's sculpture from newspaper reviewers. He now sees it as a moment when the tide began to turn towards the 'postmodernists', for him associated with artists such as Tony Cragg, Richard Deacon and Richard Wentworth, who would form the New British Sculpture at the beginning of the 1980s.

Over the same summer of Gili's show at the Serpentine, sculptures from the Depot were included in a major sculpture exhibition in Battersea Park, and in a show of St Martin's sculpture on the South Bank. Both exhibitions, as with those two years earlier, attracted harsh criticism. Simon Vaughan Winter suggested the sculptors at Greenwich and Stockwell were 'lumbering steel dinosaurs, doomed to inevitable extinction'.[78] Terence Maloon's review of the 1977 Depot exhibition, though strongly critical, was more balanced. Maloon worried that the Depot artists lacked the pragmatism, independence, vigour and freshness of their predecessors, and their 'responsiveness to the spirit of the present' – resulting in art that was 'inhibited and over-solemn'. Nevertheless he had sympathy with the underlying aims of the Depot, and suggested that in what had become a hostile climate it was no surprise that the work there had 'entrenched itself in a kind of defiant, though I suspect

73 Geoff Rigden, for example, has commented: 'Since about 1964 I'd been influenced primarily by Kenneth Noland and Morris Louis and was – if you'll pardon the expression – a Greenbergian-type painter, before I had read him closely; I'd kind of intuited what it was all about, and things evolved.' *Mali Morris interviews Geoff Rigden*, www.malimorris.co.uk/profile/texts/Geoff_Rigden_edit2014.pdf, accessed 13 April 2015.

74 Alan Gouk, 'My Relationship to American Art', unpublished.

75 The phrase 'area of competence' comes from Clement Greenberg, 'Modernist Painting', originally broadcast for *Voice of America, Form Lectures in 1960*, reprinted in Charles Harrison and Paul Wood (eds), *Art In Theory 1900–2000*, Wiley-Blackwell, Oxford, 2002, pp.773–79.

76 John McLean, introduction to *David Evison*, exhibition pamphlet, Museum of Modern Art, Oxford, 1976, n.p.

77 John Golding was one of the selectors for the *Summer Show 2* at the Serpentine Gallery, London, in 1976, in which Evison and Hide were shown; Durrant and Gili were amongst the selectors for the 1979 *Summer Show 2* which included Earley and Foster. John McLean selected the *Summer Show 2* in 1982 and included three artists associated with Stockwell – Douglas Abercrombie, Fred Pollock and Paul Tonkin – out of the ten artists he chose in total.

78 Simon Vaughan Winter thought Gili's sculptures were successful 'within the parameters of post-Caroeseque sculpture', *Artscribe*, no.7, July 1977, p.47.

provisional, conservatism. It re-mines "old-fashioned" formal concerns in a bid for a broader and hardier basis for self-renewal'. The artists were, Maloon went on, 'obliged to conserve tradition, uphold its values and standards, preserve its proscriptions, emulate the traits of its past appearances, and to do so intransigently. This is a vitally important, albeit thankless task.'[79]

With some distance from the debates of the time, it may be possible to see Stockwell Sculpture more positively. Proscriptions, intransigence, defensiveness and defiance – in short, reaction – were undoubtedly present; not just as part of a response to the current situation, but embedded within the sculptures, as part of their formal structures, of their content. Though their work developed at different rates and in different directions, across 1975 and 1976 and becoming particularly apparent in 1977 is a renewal, or at least a new and independent way of working. Important to this was a return to the body – the main focus of sculptural imagination for most of its history – which had previously underlaid sculpture's discrete existence and its interiority and separation from its immediate surroundings. Implicit across much of the Depot sculpture in the second half of the 1970s, this return was made explicit in the 1976 exhibition in Gili's *Bolero* (1976; p.113), which made a direct connection to the body in movement, or Hide's *Zenith* (1975–76; p.111) where it was figured as a stilled upright.

Where in Evison's sculpture space was given equal parity with 'stuff', in the best work of the other four, material continually intruded, bore down on space, pressurised it – at times this could lead them into a quagmire. But elsewhere the rigidity of their earlier sculpture was enlivened with a sense of animation, which could seem almost animal: not that this animation meant rigidity was done away with, but rather it slowly forced a way through constriction, occasionally erupting into something like extravagance. This can be seen in Gili's *Chillida* (1977; p.126), Foster's *Step Flashing* (1977; p.122) Hide's *High and Over* (1975–76; p.127) and Smart's series of Tamarinds (1977; p.123). The plane was the central formal device of constructed steel sculpture, which in Caro's 1960s sculpture had been freely spread across space; here it was spliced into the spatial complexity of increasingly dense sculptures, captured within a range of competing coherences. Art critic Brendan Prendeville wrote, 'the best new work proceeds slowly', suggesting the speed with which the sculptors worked through the difficult task they had set themselves, but also the mode of response their sculptures' thick plasticity engendered.[80] Though at the time the sculptors were increasingly seen as a piece, now it appears that as they drew closer together, their different artistic personalities become more distinct: Smart's based on a strange mixture of precision and a loosely ragged complexity; Hide's most involved with the definition of silhouettes and the most austere; Foster's containing the menace first noted at the Marble Hill exhibition; and Gili's most open, mobile, organic.

79 Terence Maloon, 'Painting and Sculpture at the Stockwell Depot', *Artscribe*, no.9, November, 1977, pp.44–45.

80 Brendan Prendeville, 'Constructed Sculpture', *British Sculpture in the Twentieth Century*, exhibition catalogue, Whitechapel Art Gallery, London, 1981, p.221.

Stockwell Painting

In 1976 painter Paul Tonkin replaced Geoff Rigden both in the exhibition and on the selection committee, while Jennifer Durrant, working in the Depot since 1972, had her only exhibition there. The painters in the 1977 exhibition were Gouk, McLean, Pollock and Tonkin, with McLean dropped the following year favour of Douglas Abercrombie, so that none of the painters in the 1978 exhibition had studios at the Depot. The four Scottish artists – Abercrombie, Gouk, McLean and Pollock, with McLean somewhat on the fringes of that group – as well as Tonkin, formed the core of Stockwell Painting in the last years of the 1970s. Tonkin had been taught by Rigden at Canterbury College of Art, Canterbury, and worked – as did Pollock – in a SPACE studio in Wapping. At least a decade younger than the four Scots, his painting was primarily distinguished by its undulating structures, billowing areas of rich colour contrasted with an independent, darting line. Abercrombie, whose studio was in Bombay Wharf, Rotherhithe, showed at the Depot in 1978 and 1979. At the centre of Abercrombie's painting was subtly broken colour – which could conjure naturalisitic effects from the artificial hues of acrylic paint – and a sweeping touch, which lent a sense of intimacy to even the broadest expanse.

By the mid-1970s, Durrant was working on very large-scale canvases. Her paintings were filled with soft-edged sheets of colour, forming immersive fields or coalescing into concise, frontal images. Stained paint embedded into the canvas would be added to freehand or areas scraped off to 'reveal the colour'. Although in the main employing basic geometric shapes, there

Jennifer Durrant in her studio at Stockwell Depot, London, 1979

Mark Skilton studio, Stockwell Depot, London, c.1981

Poster for *Stockwell Depot: Studio Exhibition; New Painting and Sculpture*, 1976

was – particularly in her oversized gestural marks – a hint of the figuration that would bloom in her paintings later in the decade. She wrote about her interest in 'how close up and how far away you place yourself. How much you are brought in, or feel up-against the painted surface.' Greenberg, who had continued to visit the Depot, arriving on a least a couple of occasions during these years, was impressed. Two prolonged sessions in Durrant's studio, during which he insisted she show him everything she had, may have aroused jealousy elsewhere in the studios. The visits were perhaps uncomfortable experiences for Durrant, who rarely 'had a friend or visitor to the studio. I dislike the feeling of intrusion, and like to be alone in my space.'[81] According to Evison, Greenberg went around New York telling everyone he had discovered her. Further visits followed, including from André Emmerich, a powerful dealer with galleries both sides of the Atlantic; also at this time, a painting was purchased by the Museum of Fine Arts, Boston. Greenberg wrote to McLean: 'I remain intrigued by the fact that it's the 4 Scots at Stockwell, along w. Durrant, that (as seems) are alone in England – if not in all Europe – in bearing down on painting as a high art.'[82]

Other American visitors to the Depot during these years included painters Stanley Boxer and Kenneth Noland and sculptor James Wolfe; as well as dealer Lawrence Salander and curator-critics Karen Wilkin, Ken Carpenter and Kenworth Moffett – members of the support system of an 'internationalism', based upon 'absorbing recent American developments.'[83] Greenberg wrote the introduction to the 1977 exhibition *Four Abstract Artists*, at the Fruitmarket Gallery, Edinburgh, in which Abercrombie, Gouk, McLean and Pollock were shown. He emphasised their engagement with post-painterly abstraction:

> ...un-encouraged by anything seen around in London, that is anything belonging to London. They saw how good Louis, Noland and Olitski were; they also saw – or at least John McLean did – how good Jack Bush was... What they have most in common, aside from the abstractness of their art and the North American influence, is their level, the level of their quality (which comes only in part from that influence). Otherwise they go their separate ways – not too separate, but separate enough.[84]

For Fred Pollock there were no contemporary painters in Britain 'of any quality or status or stature whatever', while 'there are five or six American painters who've done things as good as anything that's ever been painted'. McLean was more relaxed: 'They've done their paintings and we ought to be able to do ours, and still acknowledge that what they've done is good.' McLean had perhaps the widest North American contacts, and was closest to Greenberg: 'no other critic has either his energy for getting round studios or his eye for good work.' Gouk's relation to American art and its chief promoter was the most conflicted. The chief purpose behind his 1972 trip to New York had been to show a painting to Greenberg. A few years later he thought that though Greenberg was 'the only non-painter you can learn from', he had 'made one or two mistakes... that have put people on the wrong scent about where painting should be going.'[85] The intense, near-overbearing feeling Gouk brought to his paintings in the Depot exhibitions of 1975–77 were out of step with the openness and freedom that was the central expressive content of most post-painterly abstraction. Though the chief impetus behind his activity remained American in origin, the heavily worked facture which bore this feeling was bound up with an increasing engagement with European art – he remonstrated with Greenberg for tying the four Scots too tightly to post-painterly abstraction. Despite this Gouk came to adopt the technique behind his 'coal-shovel' pictures of 1978 and 1979 on a suggestion of Greenberg's, giving it up when he realised that, 'the same advice was being handed out by Clem wherever he went, Edmonton, Saskatoon, Africa, Australia.'[86]

The embrace of Hans Hofmann by painters at the Depot, particularly by Abercrombie, Gouk, Pollock, Rigden and Tonkin was in part an attempt to reconcile the scale and expansiveness of post-painterly abstraction with greater breadth and variety of colour, replacing its thinness with a more robust, heavily worked surface.[87] It was also intended to give them a more European

81 Jennifer Durrant, statement in *Hayward Annual*, exhibition catalogue, Hayward Gallery, London, 1979, n.p.

82 Clement Greenberg letter to John McLean, 10 May 1977, quoted in Ian Collins, *John McLean*, Lund Humphries, London, 2009, p.56.

83 Jennifer Durrant interview with the author, January 2015; the latter phrases come from Kenworth Moffett introduction to *The New Generation: A Curator's Choice*, exhibition catalogue, André Emmerich Gallery, New York, NY, 1980, pp.10–11.

84 Clement Greenberg, 'Four Scottish Artists', introduction to *Four Abstract Artists*, exhibition catalogue, Fruitmarket Gallery, Edinburgh, 1977, n.p.

85 The quotations in the first half of this paragraph are from Alan Gouk, Richard James, John McLean and Fred Pollock in conversation with Ben Jones, *Artscribe*, no.5, February 1977, pp.10-11.

86 Gouk, 'My Relationship to American Art', *op.cit.*

basis to their art. The painters' desire for increased physicality and complexity paralleled the sculptors' moves away from the New Generation. Likewise it went hand in hand with a move back into earlier histories of modern painting and then further into the past. In general, the painters thought the sculptors overly invested in each other's work, and conversely the sculptors that the painters were too individualist. Gouk sought to change this with the 1979 article for *Artscribe*, 'Stockwell, A Viewpoint on the Paintings'. He illustrated his and Abercrombie's paintings alongside Rubens and Claude Monet, and characterised Stockwell Painting as something with a more specific identity than a general American inheritance or a colourful supplement to the sculpture. Discussing the interaction of the Stockwell painters in the context of the Impressionists' communal formation of style, Gouk foregrounded a desire to 'allow colour maximum richness in relation to surface' through 'an engagement once again with painterly facture'.[88] Excluded from this definition of Stockwell Painting were McLean and Durrant, two painters who had studios at the Depot and, judging by sales to public collections and solo exhibitions, the two that also had the most success during the 1970s. The inventiveness and ambition with which Durrant drew on Henri Matisse's paper cut-outs is especially remote from Gouk's definition.

The final exhibition and culmination of Stockwell Sculpture

The last few years of the 1970s saw quite a lot of change in the studios. Evison had a residency in Australia in 1977. That autumn Hide moved permanently to Canada to teach, returning to Stockwell Depot to work in the summers, and entrusting the administration of his half of the Depot to Geoff Hollow. While Evison was away, his studio was taken on by sculptor David Annesley, one of the New Generation sculptors. Annesley enjoyed the studio's size and its light airiness, qualities which compensated for some of the practical difficulties working there posed: for him Evison's half contrasted with the 'gloom' of Hide's, a mood he felt reflected an increasingly 'fanatical' attention to rules for making sculpture. At the Depot, Annesley made *Fire* (1977), his contribution to the Silver Jubilee exhibition in Battersea, and for a short time after Evison returned he rented McLean's studio while the painter was away. While Hide was absent, none of the sculptors most associated with Stockwell Sculpture remained at the Depot, although there were a number of sculptors receptive to its ethos who took up spaces there, mostly students or recent graduates of the Advanced Course. Mark Skilton arrived in the Depot in 1976; Hilde Köhly in 1979. Others included Gordon Roberts, Robin Greenwood and Robert Persey, the latter two only on a temporary basis. Painter Kay Saunders took up a space in the Pillar Room in 1978, and remained until 1983, when she and Hollow moved to the Greenwich Studios. Durrant had a residency at Somerville College, Oxford in 1979, after which she moved out of the Depot.

The final Stockwell Depot annual exhibition opened in September 1979. Nineteen artists were included, nine of whom were exhibiting at the Depot for the first time: sculptors Kim Earley, Robin Greenwood, Robert Persey, Mark Skilton and Glynn Williams; painters Mick Blake, Jeff Dellow, Geoff Hollow and Mali Morris. Dellow, Morris and Persey worked at the Greenwich Studios, while Hollow and Skilton were amongst the younger artists at the Depot; Williams was head of sculpture at Wimbledon School of Art, London, where Greenwood, Hide and Smart taught. The expanded list of artists was the clearest expression of the idea, implicit from the 1975 exhibition onwards, that the Depot shows were not primarily studio exhibitions, not in the conventional sense, nor in terms of Brener's desire to work with 'particular space'. Instead, as a united front for modernist abstraction, they were a way of ensuring that artists working in increasingly apathetic or hostile conditions could have their work seen. In part this entailed giving Stockwell artists enough standing within the art world to lead to exhibitions elsewhere. More importantly it gave them control over how their work was shown, and with whom it was shown alongside. As an annually repeating event it allowed their progress to be charted against their peers, and meant their painting or sculpture could be discussed in a way not quite possible within commercial galleries or their institutional counterparts. The Depot had started as an extension of the studio situation at St Martin's, but the exhibitions were perhaps closer to a public version of the St

87 Basil Beattie, Anthony Caro, Sheila Girling, Alan Gouk, John Hoyland and Fred Pollock, 'An Interview', *Hans Hofmann: Late Paintings*, exhibition catalogue, Tate Gallery, London, 1988, pp.13–19.

88 Alan Gouk, 'Stockwell: A Viewpoint on the Paintings', *Artscribe*, no.20, November 1979, pp.16–18; Gouk also asserted, 'The sort of rivalry and mutual criticism sustained over a lifetime which enabled Pissarro, Monet, Renoir, and Cézanne to shape their respective styles… this is the sort of atmosphere we try to engender at Stockwell'.

Martin's Forums – setting up work for discussion, and also for criticism (the Depot was on occasion a site for a Forum away from the department).

Hide had been searching for an alternative venue for the Depot exhibitions since at least 1977, approaching the Hayward Gallery and Camden Arts Centre, as well as corresponding with the Storm King Art Center in New Windsor, NY about a exhibition of British and American abstract sculpture. A draft list for a proposed exhibition at the Hayward included 18 artists: among them New Generation sculptors Tim Scott and Michael Bolus, with Glynn Williams listed along with two other sculptors from Wimbledon School of Art, Ken Turnell and Lee Grandjean. The Depot exhibitions had continued to be supported by the Arts Council, also attracting funds from the Greater London Arts Association (GLAA). Grants totaling £1,050 were awarded for the Depot exhibitions in both 1977 and 1978. But as most of the work shown was brought in from elsewhere, and as increasingly heavy sculpture required a crane to get it into the Depot, the funds received for the 1978 exhibition were far short of the estimated costs, and there was no catalogue for that year. In 1977 the Arts Council warned that they could not guarantee funding in future, and the following year there were problems with funding from the GLAA. The Arts Council application for the 1979 exhibition was rejected at first. In the end the full amount of £2,050 was awarded because 'this year's exhibition was a special one and should be seen as the culmination of the preceding shows.'[89] Yet the committee did not accept that the Arts Council were obliged to continue funding the annual exhibitions. At a meeting at the beginning of 1980 most of the participants in the 1979 exhibition resolved that the shows should continue, preferably in an alternative venue and taking place within the next 18 months; the artists pledged to contribute £100 each if no funding could be found.[90] This did not come to fruition.

Painter Stuart Bradshaw thought the 1978 exhibition showed 'a feeling of complexity, experiment and confidence not felt in previous years'. Among the painters this expressed itself in a 'greater sense of freedom... shown by larger canvases and a more fluid handling of paint.' The sculpture, with the exception of that by Hide, was distinguished by an intensification of the development of the preceding years. In John Foster's sculpture this involved a greater density, with sculptures that hold themselves together like fists. The separation of planes that had been almost axiomatic within constructed steel sculpture was at least partially lost as the individual pieces of steel were increasingly mashed and melded together, through very thick welds. At times, parts seem buried within the sculptures, which can seem more carved or modelled than constructed.

A sense of carving, though without the brutality of Foster's work, was important to Gili, singled out by Stuart Bradshaw for special praise: 'Her feeling for taut, sensuous surfaces, made the sculpture feel strangely light, buoyant and rhythmic.'[91] Where Gili's and Foster's sculptures were more enclosed than the previous year, Smart's became less massive, introducing loops that pushed out into space, providing a contrast with the accumulations of steel. Hide did not share the closely worked steel of the other three, concerning himself instead with continuing the definition of silhouettes through drawing first apparent in his *Zenith*.

Yet, despite the advances made in 1978, by the following year many of the artists involved felt Stockwell Sculpture had reached something of a culmination, the consequences of which may partly explain why the annual exhibitions did not continue. Hide described the work in the expanded 1979 exhibition as 'an attempt to reconcile the profound discoveries of constructed sculpture with an awareness, at least, of the presence, sensuousness, and sheer physicality of the best sculpture of the world's past.'[92] In the exhibition catalogue artist and writer Peter Davies suggested that, 'a major breakthrough to a late twentieth-century idiom may be on the cards'.[93] In his own sculpture Hide had abandoned his planar approach, and the sculptures he exhibited, made from large slabs of steel merged together in fan-like configurations, were some of the most brutal created at the Depot. As with the previous exhibitions, there was more variety in the exhibits than many outside commentators could admit, with Foster's in particular developing from the previous year. The exhibition garnered a virulently aggressive review by Peter Fuller in *Art Monthly*. He accused the sculpture of being nothing but 'hypostasized ideology', and proceeded to

89 Letter from Joanna Drew to Peter Hide, 21 August 1979, Arts Council Archive.

90 Minutes of a meeting at the Hole in the Wall pub in Waterloo, London, 4 January 1980, Douglas Abercrombie archive. All the participants of the 1979 Depot exhibition were present except Blake, Foster, Pollock, Skilton and Williams.

91 Stuart Bradshaw, 'Stockwell Depot', *Artscribe*, no.16, February 1979, p.55.

92 Peter Hide, 'Sculpture Statement', *Stockwell Depot 12th Annual Exhibition of Painting and Sculpture*, exhibition pamphlet, Stockwell Depot, London, 1979, n.p.

93 Peter Davies, introduction to *Stockwell Depot 12th Annual Exhibition of Painting and Sculpture*, *ibid.*, n.p.

put down the painters with a series of lurid one-liners; according to Fuller, Rigden's painting was 'evocative of poached eggs in a sea of snot'.[94] This time, however, some of the sculptors felt that their work seemed to have come to halt, that it had become too large, too weighty, too unwieldy to continue with. A few years later Hide could talk of the work disparagingly as 'a massive, coagulated lumpish sort of sculpture'.[95] Gili did not feel the same way about her sculptures, which had not become as massive as those by Hide, Smart or Foster. Yet she was still involved in the dramatic changes all four made to their work at the beginning of the 1980s.

The legacy of Stockwell

The Stockwell Depot continued to be used as studio space into the early 1990s. Hide moved out for good in 1986 and Evison, although keeping on his studio, took up a teaching post in Germany. There continued to be exhibitions at the Depot, mainly in Evison's side. Like the annuals, they included a mixture of artists with studios at the Depot and those from outside, although they were smaller affairs, attracting significantly less attention. Among the younger artists who worked at Stockwell in the 1980s were Sandra Bromley, Carla Capalbo, Tim Coppard, David Gittings, Tom Grimsey, Fiona Henderson, David Kobane, Louis Maqhubela, Geoff Mowlam, David Rhodes, Marilyn Rogers and Cheron Tomkins. In 1993 Evison, Grimsey, Maqhubela and McLean relocated to studios in Oval, about a mile north of the Depot. After the last artists left, the building fell into disrepair and became a nuisance for the local community – a site for drug-taking and arson. Although there were attempts to have it protected within the Stockwell Green conversation area, it was eventually pulled down and in around 2000 was turned into flats, whose styling gestures feebly at the architectural details of the Waltham Brothers building.

The final group exhibition of Stockwell Sculpture of the 1970s took place at the Sainsbury Centre for Visual Arts in Norwich in 1982. It showed the widely divergent paths that Foster and Hide on the one hand and Smart and Gili on the other had taken in their attempts to get past the impasse presented to them by the final Depot exhibition three years earlier. Hide moved back to the planar constructed sculpture first seen in his *Zenith*, which would form the basis of the rest of his work. In more startling fashion, Foster showed a group from his series Cut-Outs (1981–82), totemic sculptures made from thick sections of pipe, minimally worked into stark, simple silhouettes. Though the verticality of the sculptures by Foster and Hide contained a reference to the body, the two sculptures by Gili and Smart were literally figures, with arms and legs held in difficult positions, described in heavily worked forged steel – Gili's lithe, Smart's bulkier, made from great globules of steel.

Over the course of an intensive and controversial few years, the St Martin's sculpture department, under Tim Scott and Alan Gouk, had been transformed. The planar constructed tradition had been rejected and, using life models, the body made the subject of prolonged scrutiny, in an endeavour to 'find a true principle of unity and one which offers the same degree of intensity as pertained in our identification with bodily relationships'.[96] The origins of 'sculpture from the body' lay in Tucker's writing and in Scott's sculpture, but it was also bound up with Stockwell Sculpture, in its intensely serious, narrow focus and the willingness of individuals involved to work communally. Sculptures from the tendency were exhibited at Tate in 1984 and in Spain in 1988, by which time most of the artists had taken their experiments with the body back into abstraction.[97]

The legacy of painting at the Depot continued in Kenworth Moffett's 1980 exhibition, *The New Generation: A Curator's Choice* at André Emmerich Gallery, New York, in which Abercrombie, Durrant and McLean were shown alongside other international examples of painters working out of post-painterly abstraction. Abercrombie and Pollock were included in an exhibition in Poole curated by Peter Davies. Gouk and Rigden exhibited together in 1982 at the Woodlands Gallery in Greenwich. Most prominent was the *Hayward Annual* of 1980, selected by painter John Hoyland, which included six painters who had worked or shown at the Depot. In the catalogue, critic Tim Hilton – a regular visitor to the Depot – suggested it was the 'dismal setting' in

94 Peter Fuller, 'Stockwell Depot', *Art Monthly*, no.30, October, 1979, pp.14–17.
95 Peter Hide, *Sculpture from Stockwell Depot*, exhibition catalogue, Sainsbury Centre for Visual Arts, Norwich, 1982, p.1
96 Gouk, 'Proper to Sculpture', *op.cit.*, p.12.

97 *Have You Seen Sculpture From the Body?*, exhibition catalogue, Tate Gallery, London, 1984; Escultura Nueva Reino Unido, Conde Duque, Madrid, 1988.

Installation view, *Sculpture from Stockwell Depot*, Sainsbury Centre for Visual Arts, Norwich, 1982

Left to right:
Anthony Smart, *1st Figure* (1980–82); Peter Hide, *Wall to Wall* (1981); John Foster, sculpture from the Cut-Outs series (1981–83); Hide, *Beat Bush Revisited* and *Nordelph Cornucopia* (both 1981); Katherine Gili, *Leonide* (1981–82); Hide, *British Standard* and *Procession* (both 1981); Foster, sculpture from the Cut-Outs series (1981–83)

which, at the 'nadir' of its public fortunes, the painting tradition had gone underground:

> How little it was appreciated five or six years ago, and how unworldly were its aspirations, prompts me to say something about what was called its conservatism. For far from being conservative, it was considered by its authors as being – within the general context of culture – radical; not that it wished to change society or to reflect society, but that it stood for things – was those things – otherwise unvalued. It was a force against the basilisk, and yet not a force: only itself.[98]

Frank Bowling put similar thoughts in a more straight-forward fashion three years later: 'This multiple work space – and there are others in Wapping, Greenwich and elsewhere – contributed some of the lively energy that sustains British painting and sculpture, not the market, despite the talk of our living in a market economy.'[99]

Some of the Stockwell artists would continue to work in close quarters at Greenwich or at its successor at APT (Art in Perpetuity Trust) in Deptford; some attended the early iterations of the Triangle Workshops in New York State or the Hardingham Workshops in rural Norfolk, which Foster founded in 1986 in response to his experiences at Triangle. Yet these later examples of communal endeavour did not involve the public assertion of the Depot exhibitions, or at least were ignored by the wider art world. Despite their prominence in the 1970s, Stockwell sculptors have been excluded from almost all publications and exhibitions surveying the period, or from wider accounts of British sculpture. Since that time, their achievements have been largely individual. Gili and Smart, along with a number of the other sculptors associated with 'sculpture from the body' developed what should be recognised as an innovative form of (late, late) modern sculpture, based upon their work at the Depot in the 1970s but differing significantly from it. Hide and Evison have both developed substantial bodies of work and reputations as teachers in Canada and Germany respectively. By the early 1980s, Greenberg thought Hide 'one of the three or four best sculptors working anywhere right now' and by 1991, placed him second only to Caro,[100] yet the upright sculptures that Hide has made since the mid-1970s – the most direct continuation of Stockwell Sculpture by any of the artists – have not been properly shown *en masse* in Britain. Many painters associated with the Depot have experienced similar difficulties. Tim Hilton claimed Hoyland's *Hayward Annual* of 1980 as the most important exhibition in Britain since *Situation* at RBA Gallery (Royal Society of British Artists), London in 1960, but where that exhibition had marked the beginning of a vigorous period of invention in abstract painting, the Hayward show seems to mark a point of closure, after which the artists involved were excluded from the dominant discourse around the medium.[101] The narrative of the return to painting of the 1980s had no room for the artists who had been involved with it through the previous decade, and was primarily concerned with figuration not abstraction.

This marginalisation was undeserved, and contributed to Stockwell Depot being denied its rightful place within the contested history of art in late 1960s and 70s Britain; a situation which is beginning to be rectified. More importantly still, the work – the sculpture in particular – which was made and shown there and has continued to develop since, should be considered for its own sake and incorporated into wider narratives of modernist abstraction.

98 Tim Hilton, 'A Force Against the Basilisk', *Hayward Annual 1980: Contemporary Painting and Sculpture Selected by John Hoyland*, exhibition catalogue, Hayward Gallery, London, 1980, p.9.
99 Frank Bowling, 'Notes Along the Way', *Fuse*, autumn, 1988, p.4.
100 Letter from Clement Greenberg to Professor Chenier, July 1983, Peter Hide archive; *Interview with Clement Greenberg*, The Edmonton Contemporary Artists Society Newsletter, vol.3, no.2, 1991, see http://www.sharecom.ca/greenberg/interview.html, accessed 14 April 2015.
101 Hilton, *op.cit.*

David Evison
Untitled, 1982
Steel
Height: 170 cm | 66⅞ in

Peter Hide
Rondour, 1984–86
Rusted mild steel
257 × 96 × 56 cm | 101⅛ × 37¾ × 22⅛ in

Work from Stockwell Depot 1967–79

**Editors' note:
Structured around the pivotal annual exhibitions, this section illustrates work that was made, installed, or exhibited at Stockwell Depot during this period.**

1967–68

Stockwell Depot: Sculpture Exhibition

Alan Barkley
Roland Brener
David Evison
Roger Fagin
John Fowler
Gerard Hemsworth
Peter Hide
Roelof Louw

Roelof Louw
Ring I, c.1967

Iron, steel
1.3 × 4.2 m | 3¼ × 10½ ft
Stockwell Depot: Sculpture Exhibition,
Stockwell Depot, London, 1968

Roland Brener
Bow Sculpture, 1968

Painted steel, tensile wire
1.2 × 14.3 × 2.3 m | 4 × 47 × 7½ ft
Stockwell Depot: Sculpture Exhibition,
Stockwell Depot, London, 1968

Roland Brener
Sculpture with Four Arches, 1968

Steel, iron, concrete
2.1 × 12.2 × 6.1 m | 7 × 39¼ × 20 ft
Stockwell Depot: Sculpture Exhibition,
Stockwell Depot, London, 1968

Roland Brener
Sculpture with Single Arch, 1968

Steel, iron, concrete
2.7 × 6.1 × 3.7 m | 9 × 20 × 12 ft
Stockwell Depot: Sculpture Exhibition,
Stockwell Depot, London, 1968

David Evison
Sculpture II, 1968

Painted wood
Height: 2.2 m | 7 ft (approx.)
Stockwell Depot, London

Gerard Hemsworth
While, 1968

Wood, plastic
0.5 × 2.4 × 2.7 m | 1½ × 8 × 9 ft (approx.)
Stockwell Depot, London

Installation view, *Stockwell Depot: Sculpture Exhibition*, Stockwell Depot, London, 1968
with Alan Barkley, *Brown Piece* (1968; foreground) and works by John Fowler and Gerard Hemsworth

Installation view, *Stockwell Depot: Sculpture Exhibition*, Stockwell Depot, London, 1968
with works by David Evison and Roger Fagin

Peter Hide
Red Fence, 1968 (left)

Bolted and painted mild steel
2.4 × 3.7 × 4.3 m | 8 × 12 × 14 ft (approx.)

Blue Posts, 1968 (right)

Bolted and painted mild steel
3.2 × 3 × 1.8 m | 10½ × 10 × 6 ft (approx.)
Stockwell Depot, London

Roger Fagin
Untitled, 1968

Railway sleepers, steel
3 × 6 × 5 m | 16½ × 19½ × 19 ft (approx.)
Stockwell Depot, London

Roger Fagin
Untitled, 1968

Painted steel
2.4 × 4 × 2.4 m | 8 × 13 × 8 ft (approx.)

Shirley Cameron
Troika, 1967

Painted wood
1.8 × 5.5 × 3.7 m | 6 × 18 × 12 ft
Sculpture in the City, City of London Festival, London, 1968

1969

Stockwell Depot 2: Sculpture

Alan Barkley
Roland Brener
David Evison
Roger Fagin
John Fowler
Gerard Hemsworth
Peter Hide
Roelof Louw
Rita Marshall

David Evison
Flag Sculpture, 1969

Painted steel
Height: 3.2 m | 10½ ft
Stockwell Depot, London

Roger Fagin
Untitled, 1969

Railway sleepers
Dimensions variable
Stockwell Depot 2: Sculpture, Stockwell Depot,
London, 1969

Roelof Louw
Rope Sculpture, 1969

Rope
Dimensions variable
Stockwell Depot 2: Sculpture, Stockwell Depot, London, 1969

Roelof Louw
Untitled, c.1968

Painted and sand-blasted aluminium
Dimensions unknown
Stockwell Depot, London

Roland Brener
Sculpture with Three Bows, 1969

Painted steel, wire, iron
0.8 × 15.2 × 1.5 m | 2½ × 50 × 5 ft
Stockwell Depot 2: Sculpture, Stockwell Depot, London, 1969

Installation views,
Stockwell Depot, London, 1969
with works by Gerard
Hemsworth

John Fowler
Jelly Roll, 1969

Painted fibreglass
0.9 × 2.7 × 0.9 m | 3 × 9 × 3 ft
Stockwell Depot, London

Alan Barkley
Marion's Window, c.1969

Painted plywood
2.1 × 2.1 × 2.1 m | 7 × 7 × 7 ft (approx.)
Stockwell Depot, London

John McLean
1969, 1969

Acrylic on canvas
162.9 × 40.3 cm | 64⅛ × 15⅞ in

Gary Wragg
Salmon Pink Interior, 1968

Acrylic on canvas
102 × 76 cm | 40⅛ × 29⅞ in

Installation view, Stockwell Depot, London, 1969
with components for Roland Brener, Tubular Sculpture series (1969)

Roland Brener
Tubular Sculpture #1, 1969

Painted steel
2.7 × 3.1 × 4.6 m | 9 × 10 × 15 ft (approx.)
Stockwell Depot, London

Installation view, *New Sculpture 1969*, Stevenage, 1969 with Roland Brener, *Untitled* (1969; left) and Peter Hide, *Untitled* (1969; right)

1970

Stockwell Depot: Peter Hide, Roland Brener: An Independent Exhibition

Roland Brener
Peter Hide

Roland Brener
Deep Space Installation, 1970

Nylon cord, balsa wood
6.1 × 9.1 × 3.1 m | 20 × 30 × 10 ft
Stockwell Depot: Eight English Sculptors from London, Konsthallen, Gothenburg, 1970

Installation view, *Stockwell Depot: Peter Hide, Roland Brener: An Independent Exhibition*, Stockwell Depot, London, 1970

Left to right:
Peter Hide, *Plateau*; *Tower* and *Tank* (all 1969–70)

Installation view, *Stockwell Depot: Peter Hide, Roland Brener: An Independent Exhibition*, Stockwell Depot, London, 1970
with Peter Hide, *Tripod* (1970; left) and *Pyramid* (1968-69; right)

Roland Brener
Black Light Installation, 1970

Fluorescent fishing line, ultraviolet light
7.9 × 7.9 m | 26 × 26 ft
Stockwell Depot: Peter Hide, Roland Brener: An Independent Exhibition, Stockwell Depot, London, 1970

Roland Brener
Black Light Space Installation, 1970

Fluorescent fishing line, ultraviolet light
7.9 × 15.2 m | 25 × 50 ft
Stockwell Depot: Peter Hide, Roland Brener: An Independent Exhibition, Stockwell Depot, London, 1970

Installation view, *Stockwell Depot: Eight English Sculptors from London*, Kunstnernes Hus, Oslo, 1970 with works by Roland Brener and Gerard Hemsworth

Installation view, *Stockwell Depot: Eight English Sculptors from London*, Kunstnernes Hus, Oslo, 1970

Left to right:
Peter Hide, *Pyramid* (1968–69); Alan Barkley, *Marion's Window* (c.1969); David Evison, *Flag Sculpture* and *Solo Track* (both 1969)

Installation view, *Stockwell Depot: Eight English Sculptors from London*, Konsthallen, Gothenburg, 1970
with Peter Hide, *Pyramid* (1968–69; background); Roelof Louw, *Untitled* (c.1968; right); and works by Gerard Hemsworth and Roelof Louw

Roland Brener
Rod and Wire Sculpture with Suspended Objects, 1970

Fishing rods, iron, plaster ducks, wire
2.7 × 3.7 × 6.1 m | 8¾ × 12¼ × 20 ft

David Evison

3 Levels, 1970

Steel
Height: 3.2 m | 10½ ft
David Evison, Kasmin Limited, London, 1970

Patagonia, 1970

Steel
Height: 2.9 m | 9½ ft
David Evison, Kasmin Limited, London, 1970

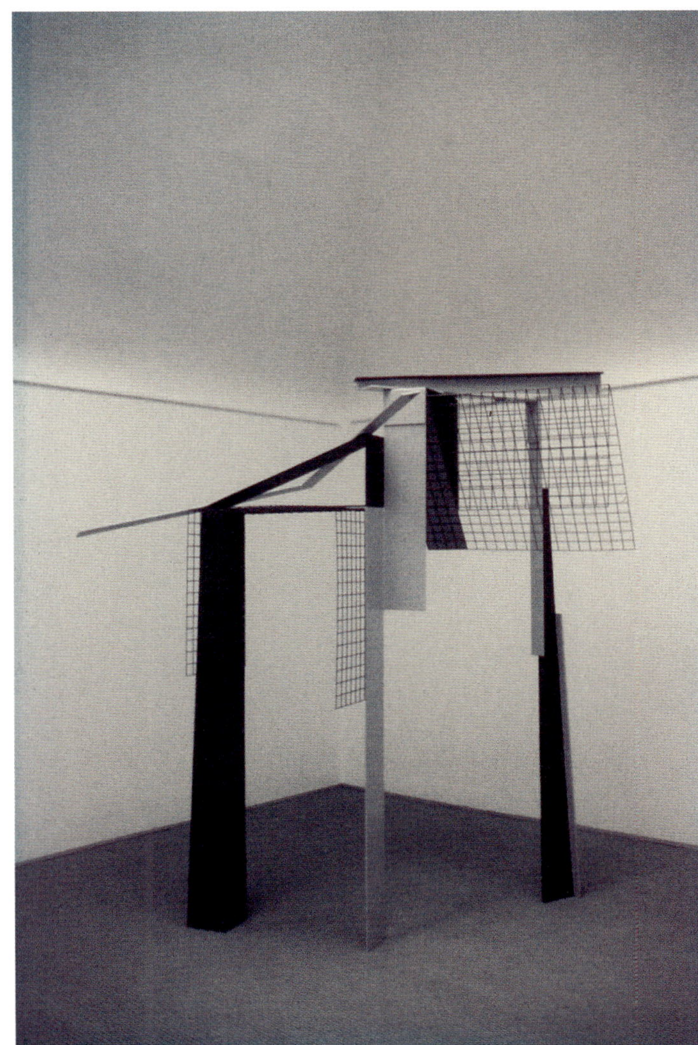

1971

Stockwell Depot: Peter Hide: An Independent Exhibition

Peter Hide

Peter Hide
Arch, 1971

Galvanised and painted mild steel, concrete
5.3 × 25 × 1.1 m | 17½ × 82 × 3½ ft
Carletonville, South Africa

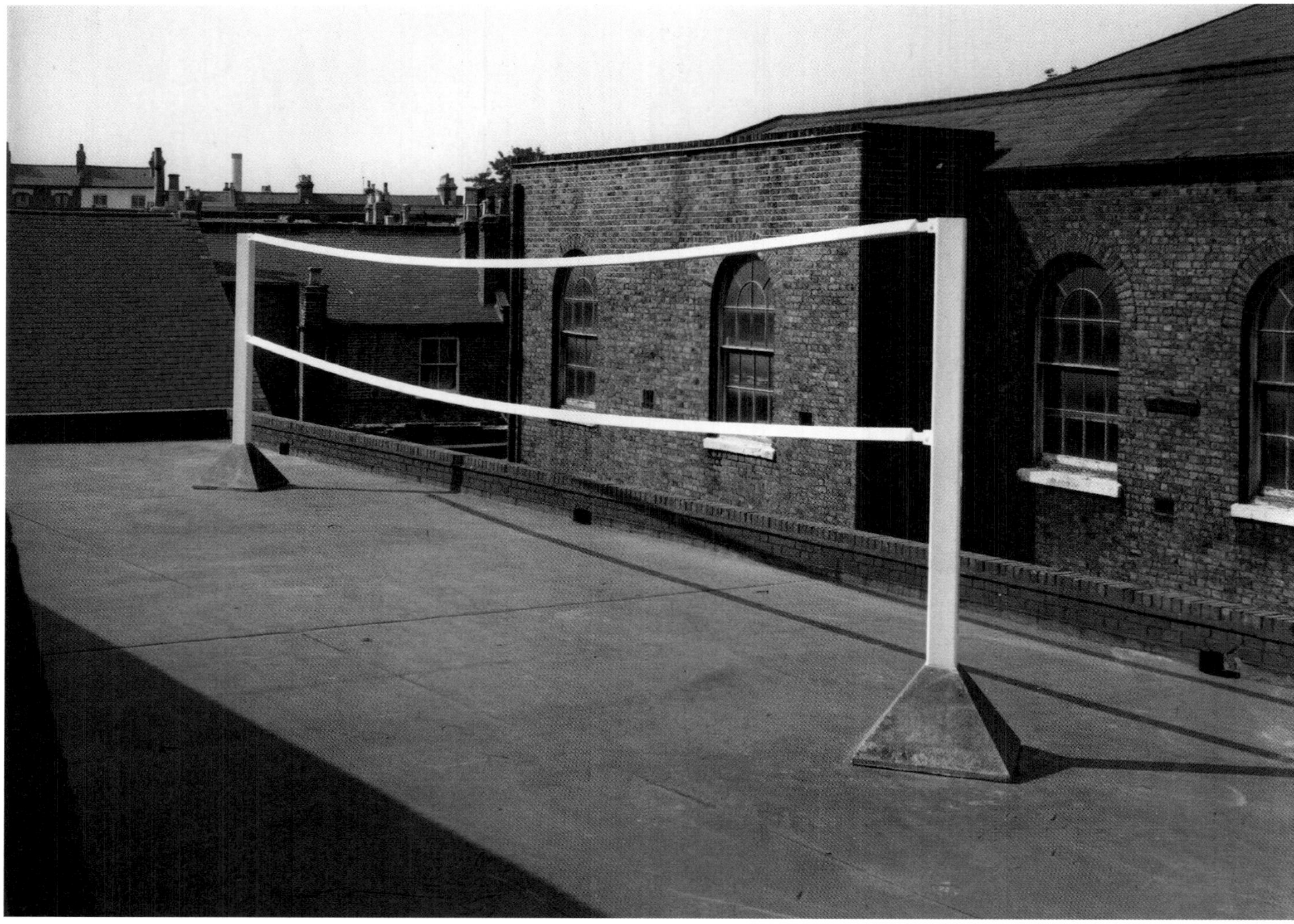

Peter Hide
36 Foot Span, 1971

Painted mild steel, concrete
2.8 × 12.8 × 1.1 m | 9⅛ × 42 × 3⅝ ft
Stockwell Depot: Peter Hide: An Independent Exhibition, Stockwell Depot, London, 1971

Peter Hide
Sculpture Number 3, 1971

Painted mild steel, concrete
2.6 × 6.5 × 0.8 m | 8.5 × 21⅛ × 2½ ft
Stockwell Depot: Peter Hide: An Independent Exhibition, Stockwell Depot, London, 1971

John McLean
Penicuik, Midlothian, 1971

PVA emulsion on canvas
152.5 × 335 cm | 60⅛ × 131⅞ in

John Golding
A III, 1971

Acrylic on canvas
213 × 457 cm | 83⅞ × 179⅞ in

1972

Stockwell Depot: Peter Hide, Sculpture; Richard James, Paintings

Peter Hide
Richard James

John McLean
Number One (Vertical Painting), 1972

PVA emulsion on canvas
273 × 152.5 cm | 107½ × 60⅛ in

David Evison
Irrawaddy, 1971

Painted steel, wood
2.9 × 2.2 × 1.8 m | 9½ × 7 × 6 ft
David Evison: Recent Sculptures, Kasmin Limited, London, 1972

Right:
Peter Hide
Compression Pillar, 1972

Concrete, iron
Height: 4 m | 13 ft
City Sculpture Project, Guildhall Square, Southampton, 1972

1973

Stockwell Depot: Peter Hide, Sculpture; Richard James, Paintings

Peter Hide
Richard James

John Foster
Frame III, 1973

Steel, concrete
2.7 × 2.8 × 0.9 m | 9 × 9½ × 3 ft
John Foster and Peter Hide, Marble Hill House, London, 1973

John Foster
Slab Sculpture III, 1973

Steel, concrete
0.9 × 3.7 × 2.3 m | 3 × 12 × 7½ ft
John Foster and Peter Hide, Marble Hill House, London, 1973

Installation view, *John Foster and Peter Hide*, Marble Hill House, London, 1973 with John Foster, *Slab Sculpture II* (1973; foreground) and works by John Foster and Peter Hide

Peter Hide
Trapezium, 1973

Steel, concrete
2.7 × 12.5 × 0.8 m | 9 × 34½ × 2½ ft
John Foster and Peter Hide, Marble Hill House, London, 1973

1974

Stockwell Depot: New Sculpture

John Foster
Katherine Gili
Peter Hide
Anthony Smart

Peter Hide
Advance, 1974

Painted mild steel
3.4 × 2.8 × 1.5 m | 11 × 9 × 5 ft
Stockwell Depot: New Sculpture, Stockwell Depot, London, 1974

MOTOR INSU

Peter Hide
Broadside, 1974

Painted mild steel
61 × 151 × 100 cm | 24⅛ × 59½ × 39⅜ in
Stockwell Depot: New Sculpture, Stockwell Depot, London, 1974

John Foster
Small Drum, 1974

Steel
69 × 61 × 61 cm | 27⅛ × 24⅛ × 24⅛ in
Stockwell Depot, London

John Foster
Blue Drum, 1974

Painted steel
2.6 × 1.3 × 1.3 m | 8½ × 4½ × 4½ ft
Stockwell Depot, London

Anthony Smart
Large Curve, 1974

Mild steel
Height: 152.4 cm | 60 in
Stockwell Depot, London

Katherine Gili
Cut, 1974

Mild steel
173 × 164 × 110 cm | 68 × 64½ × 43¼ in
Stockwell Depot: New Sculpture, Stockwell Depot, London, 1974

Left to right:
John Foster, *Small Ring*; *Small Drum IV*; *Small Drum III* and *Small Drum* (all 1974)

Katherine Gili
Splay, 1974

Mild steel
137 × 115 × 107 cm | 54 × 45¼ × 42⅛ in
Stockwell Depot, London

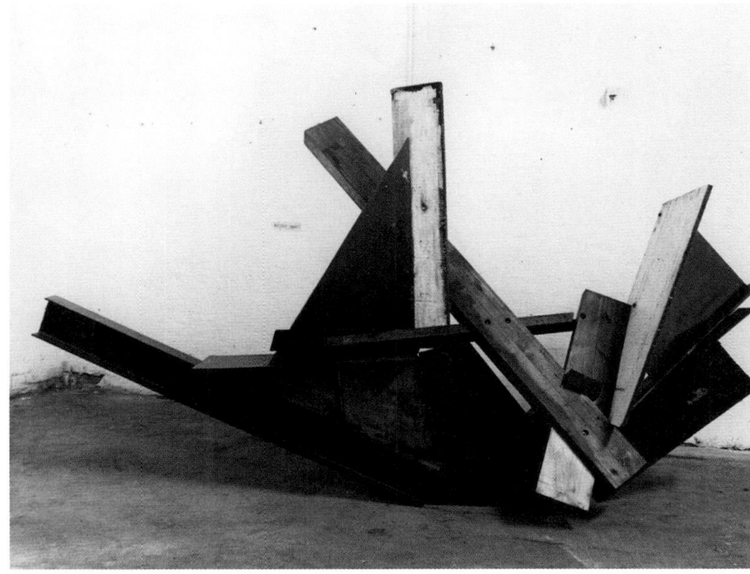

Anthony Smart
Windjammer, 1974

Steel, wood
Height: 182.9 cm | 72 in
Stockwell Depot, London

David Evison
No.II, 1974

Steel, aluminium
Height: 2.2 m | 7 ft (approx.)
Stockwell Depot, London

1975

Stockwell Depot: Studio Exhibition; New Painting and Sculpture

Stephenie Bergman
David Evison
John Foster
Katherine Gili
Alan Gouk
Peter Hide
John McLean
Fred Pollock
Geoff Rigden
Anthony Smart

Katherine Gili
Vertical IV, 1975

Zinc-sprayed and painted mild steel
2.2 × 1.6 × 1.1 m | 7½ × 5 × 3½ ft

Fred Pollock
Olive Keeker, 1975

Acrylic on canvas
203.2 × 76.2 cm | 80 × 30 in

Right:
Peter Hide
Much Longer, 1975

Painted and varnished mild steel
84 × 330 × 111 cm | 33 × 130 × 44 in
Stockwell Depot: Studio Exhibition: New Painting and Sculpture, Stockwell Depot, London, 1975 with Alan Gouk, *Chardin's Nose* (1973; left) and Fred Pollock, *Olive Keeker* (1975; right)

David Evison
Untitled, 1975

Steel, aluminium
Height: 2.8 m | 9 ft
Stockwell Depot: Studio Exhibition; New Painting and Sculpture, Stockwell Depot, London, 1975

John McLean
Pagoda I, 1975

Acrylic on canvas
186 × 97 cm | 73¼ × 38¼ in

Peter Hide
Sodium, 1975

Steel
129 × 101 × 61 cm | 50 × 39¾ × 28 in
Summer Show 2, Serpentine Gallery, London, 1976

Right:
Alan Gouk
Unstern – Pianistic Shudder, 1975

Acrylic on flax
199 × 153 cm | 78⅜ × 60¼ in

Stephenie Bergman
Blind Venetian, 1975

Paint and dye on canvas
196 × 196 cm | 77⅛ × 77⅛ in

Geoff Rigden
Natty Dread, 1975–76

Acrylic on canvas
204 × 107 cm | 80¼ × 42⅛ in

1976

Stockwell Depot: Studio Exhibition;
New Painting and Sculpture

Jennifer Durrant
Katherine Gili
Alan Gouk
Peter Hide
John McLean
Fred Pollock
Anthony Smart
Paul Tonkin

Peter Hide
Zenith, 1975–76

Welded and rusted mild steel
3 × 1 × 0.5 m | 9½ × 3½ × 2 ft
Stockwell Depot, London

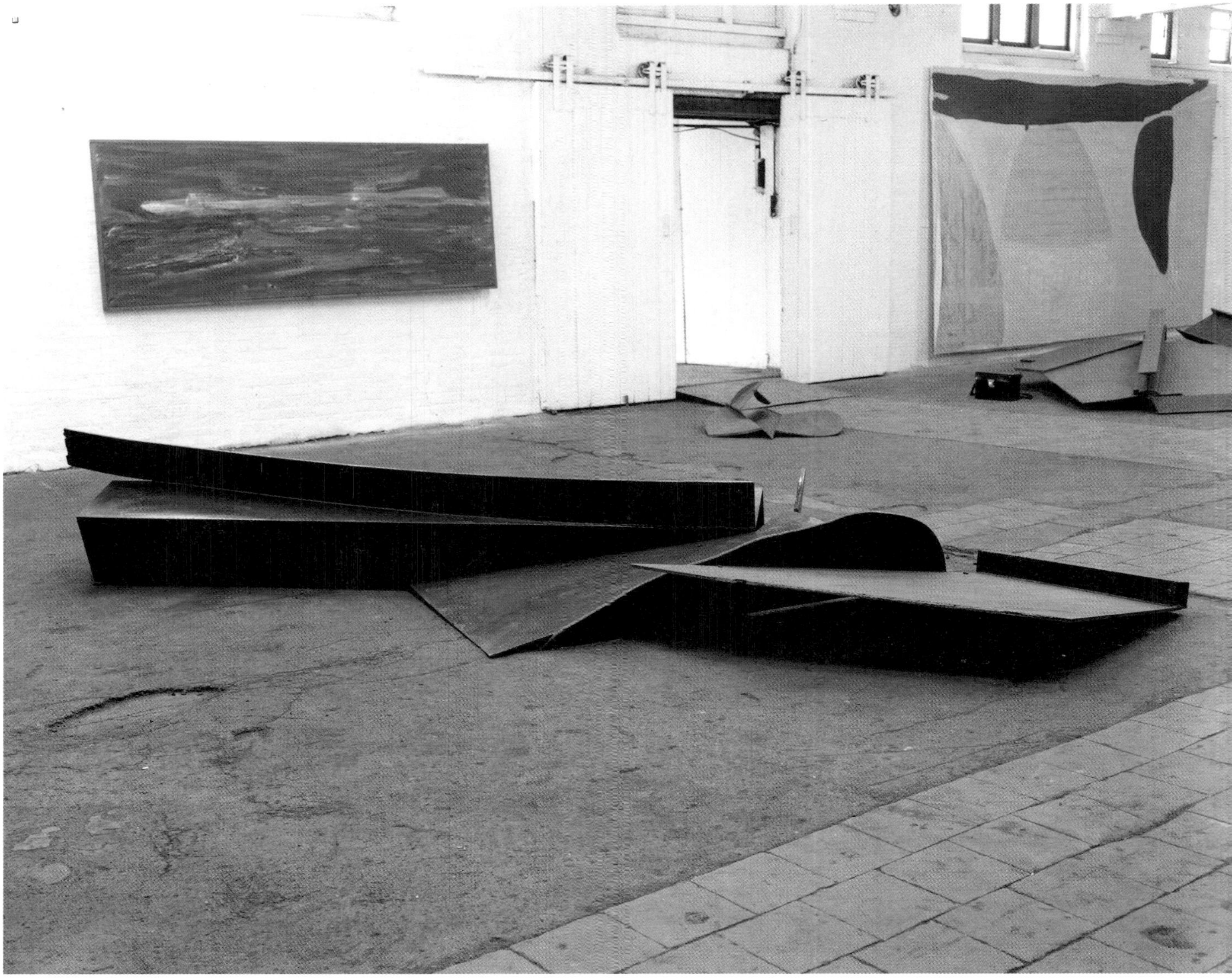

Peter Hide
Sea Plane, 1976

Mild steel
0.6 × 4.5 × 2.8 m | 2 × 15 × 9 ft
Stockwell Depot: Studio Exhibition; New Painting and Sculpture, Stockwell Depot, London, 1976 with Alan Gouk, *Mona Pressure* (1976; left) and work by Jennifer Durrant (c.1975–76; right)

Right:
Katherine Gili
Bolero, 1976

Varnished mild steel
2.3 × 1.3 × 0.7 m | 7½ × 4 × 2½ ft
Stockwell Depot: Studio Exhibition; New Painting and Sculpture, Stockwell Depot, London, 1976

Anthony Smart
Untitled, 1976

Mild steel
Height: 137.2 cm | 54 in
Stockwell Depot: Studio Exhibition; New Painting and Sculpture, Stockwell Depot, London, 1976

Anthony Smart
Untitled, 1976

Mild steel
Height: 152.4 cm | 60 in
Stockwell Depot: Studio Exhibition; New Painting and Sculpture, Stockwell Depot, London, 1976

Jennifer Durrant
First Yellow Painting, 1975

Acrylic on canvas
265.4 × 358.1 cm | 104½ × 141 in

Peter Hide
Pomeroy, 1974–75

Rusted mild steel
1.8 × 4 × 3 m | 6 × 13 × 10 ft
Summer Show 2, Serpentine Gallery, London, 1976

David Evison
Untitled, 1976

Steel
2.4 × 2.3 × 2.2 m | 8 × 7½ × 7½ ft
David Evison, Museum of Modern Art, Oxford, 1976

Paul Tonkin
Lair, 1976

Acrylic on canvas
174 × 114 cm | 68½ × 44⅞ in

1977

Stockwell Depot: 10th Anniversary Exhibition of New Sculpture and Painting

John Foster
Katherine Gili
Alan Gouk
Peter Hide
John McLean
Fred Pollock
Anthony Smart
Paul Tonkin

Alan Gouk
Skoochai, 1976

Oil on linen
263 × 147 cm | 103½ × 57⅞ in

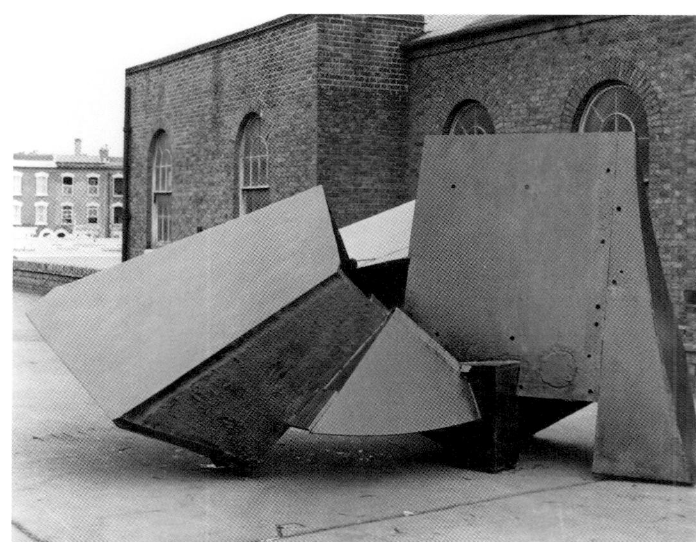

John Foster
Step Flashing, 1977

Steel
Height: 177 cm | 69¾ in
Stockwell Depot: 10th Anniversary Exhibition of New Sculpture and Painting, Stockwell Depot, London, 1977

Anthony Smart
Tamarind X, 1977

Mild steel
1.6 × 1.6 × 1.5 m | 5½ × 5½ × 5 ft
Stockwell Depot: 10th Anniversary Exhibition of New Sculpture and Painting, Stockwell Depot, London, 1977

Paul Tonkin
Something, 1976–77

Acrylic on canvas
184 × 138 cm | 72½ × 54⅜ in

Fred Pollock
Honeydripper, 1977

Acrylic on canvas
165 × 293 cm | 65 × 115⅜ in

Katherine Gili
Chillida, 1977

Varnished mild steel
160 × 148 × 110 cm | 63 × 58¼ × 43¼ in
Summer Show 2, Serpentine Gallery, London, 1977

Katherine Gili
Roundelay, 1977

Varnished mild steel
125 × 154 × 114 cm | 49¼ × 60½ × 44¾ in
Summer Show 2, Serpentine Gallery, London, 1977

David Evison

Untitled, 1977

Steel
Height: 2.8 m | 9¼ ft
St Martin's South Bank Sculpture, South Bank, London, 1977

Installation view, *St Martin's South Bank Sculpture*, South Bank, London, 1977 with Peter Hide, *Pomeroy* (1974–75; left) and *High and Over* (1975–76; right)

1978

11th Annual Stockwell Depot Exhibition: Sculpture and Painting

Douglas Abercrombie
John Foster
Katherine Gili
Alan Gouk
Peter Hide
Fred Pollock
Anthony Smart
Paul Tonkin

Douglas Abercrombie
Untitled, c.1977–78

Acrylic and sand on canvas
172.7 × 370.8 cm | 68 × 146 in (approx.)

Installation views, *11th Annual Stockwell Depot Exhibition: Sculpture and Painting*, Stockwell Depot, London, 1978

Top left:
Anthony Smart, *Stirrup 1* (1978; foreground) and Douglas Abercrombie, *Untitled* (c.1977–79; background)

Top right:
Katherine Gili, *Hug* (1978; foreground) and Douglas Abercrombie, *Untitled*, (1978; background)

Bottom left:
Peter Hide, *Rondo* (1978; foreground)

Bottom right:
Sculpture by Peter Hide (foreground) and Alan Gouk, *Untitled* (1978; background)

Right:
John Foster
Full Face, 1978 (modified, 1979)

Steel
168 × 92 × 92 cm | 66 × 36 × 36 in
11th Annual Stockwell Depot Exhibition: Sculpture and Painting, Stockwell Depot, London, 1978

Anthony Smart
Stirrup 1, 1978

Mild steel
Height: 91.4 cm | 36 in

Katherine Gili
Blow, 1978 (modified, 1979)

Waxed mild steel
164 × 90 × 87 cm | 64½ × 39 × 34¼ in

Alan Gouk
Wild Orchid, 1978

Acrylic on cotton duck
203 × 169 cm | 79⅞ × 66½ in

Peter Hide
Rondo, 1978

Rusted mild steel
2.1 × 1.4 × 0.6 m | 7 × 4½ × 2 ft

1979

Stockwell Depot: 12th Annual Exhibition of Painting and Sculpture

Douglas Abercrombie
Mick Blake
Jeff Dellow
Kim Earley
John Foster
Katherine Gili
Alan Gouk
Robin Greenwood
Peter Hide
Geoff Hollow
John McLean
Mali Morris
Robert Persey
Fred Pollock
Geoff Rigden
Mark Skilton
Anthony Smart
Paul Tonkin
Glynn Williams

Anthony Smart
Untitled, 1979

Mild steel
Height: 111.8 cm | 44 in

John Foster
Back Break, 1979

Steel
135 × 90 × 83 cm | 53⅛ × 35⅜ × 32⅝ in (approx.)
Summer Show 2, Serpentine Gallery, London, 1979

Katherine Gili
Rise, 1979

Waxed mild steel
90 × 98 × 60 cm | 35½ × 38½ × 23⅝ in

Alan Gouk
In the Wake of the Plough, 1979

Acrylic on cotton duck
175 × 124 cm | 68⅞ × 48⅞ in

Mark Skilton
Untitled, 1979

Mild steel
128 × 110 × 88 cm | 50⅜ × 43¼ × 34⅝ in
Stockwell Depot: 12th Annual Exhibition of Painting and Sculpture, Stockwell Depot, London, 1979

Robert Persey
79 Piece, 1979

Mild steel
96 × 105 × 63 cm | 37 ¾ × 41⅜ × 24¾ in
Woodlands Gallery, London

Peter Hide
Left Arm Chinaman, 1979

Welded mild steel
189 × 131 × 170 cm | 74⅜ × 51⅝ × 66⅞ in

Mali Morris
Second Party, 1979

Acrylic and oil on canvas
180 × 180 cm | 70⅞ × 70⅞ in

Jeff Dellow
Ascent, 1979

Acrylic on canvas
228 × 165 cm | 89¾ × 65 in

Douglas Abercrombie
Dun Column, 1979

Acrylic on canvas
182 × 70 cm | 71⅝ × 27½ in

Fred Pollock
Yellow Vision, 1979

Acrylic on canvas
165 × 103 cm | 65 × 40½ in

Geoff Hollow
Jaws, 1980

Acrylic on canvas
152.4 × 114.3 cm | 60 × 45 in

Installation view, *Jennifer Durrant: Paintings 1976–79*, Arnolfini Gallery, Bristol, 1979 with works by Jennifer Durrant including *Sweet Pea Painting* (1978–79; left)

Geoff Rigden
Little Rootie Tootie, 1978–79

Acrylic and oil on canvas
42 × 109 cm | 16½ × 42⅞ in

John McLean
Kilmahoe, 1979

Acrylic on cotton duck
213.5 × 165 cm | 84⅛ × 65 in

David Evison, Gerard Hemsworth, Roland Brener, Roelof Louw, Peter Hide, Roger Fagin and John Fowler, Stockwell Depot, London, 1968

Reflections on Stockwell Depot

Interviews by Sam Cornish and David Waterworth

Editors' note:
The following text combines selected extracts from interviews held separately, between 2013–14, with ten of the artists associated with Stockwell Depot. The selection addresses core issues associated with the Depot during 1967–79, a period in which each of these artists had an active involvement. David Evison, Gerard Hemsworth and Peter Hide helped to set up the studios in 1967; John McLean moved into an area managed by Evison by 1970; Jennifer Durrant, Katherine Gili and Anthony Smart all first sublet from Hide in the early 1970s; and Mark Skilton arrived later in that decade. From 1975–79 the annual Stockwell Depot exhibitions regularly included a number of artists, including Alan Gouk and Paul Tonkin, who did not have studio spaces in the building.

Establishing the Depot

Peter Hide None of us knew what we were going to do in terms of where to work after St Martin's. It was like a sort of precipice that was rapidly approaching. Roland Brener and I were contemporaries there and we talked a lot about forming a group, but it was a nebulous sort of idea. Roland, who lived in Lambeth at the time, approached Lambeth Council and the borough valuer came up with this old, unoccupied property that had been built and used as a brewery, then a warehouse. Pride and Clarke, the motorbike people, had used it. Roland took the lease for the second floor initially, sometime in June or July 1967.

David Evison We were St Martin's ex-sculpture students, all leaving at about the same time. The building was too big for Roland Brener. He was only interested in one particular area – there were two or three areas available – so he informed me about it and he informed Gerard Hemsworth, who took an area of small rooms and I had the large area to deal with.

Gerard Hemsworth I graduated from St Martin's in 1967 and was looking for a studio to work in. Roland Brener, who graduated the year before me, had found this large disused property in Stockwell and was in discussion with Lambeth Council. He asked me if I was interested, so I also contacted Lambeth; there were a group of smaller spaces in the building – probably the offices – which I eventually took responsibility for.

Roland convinced Lambeth Council that they should support the arts, and had made a deal with them regarding rent. I can't remember exactly what the deal was – it may have been that we were not paying rates – but whatever it was, it meant that the studios were extremely affordable. In 1967, Roland Brener with Peter Hide, Roger Fagin and Roelof Louw took one section of the building; I took the offices and David Evison took on another area.

Developments in the 1970s

Peter Hide In 1970 Nigel Greenwood arranged for us to get a British Council touring exhibition in Scandinavia. The group held together for that but afterwards we essentially broke up. David Evison remained with his west wing, and he took in the painter John McLean. Roland Brener and I remained fast friends, but he went off for a year to teach in the US so I was essentially left alone in the big part of the space. Then Roland came back and we showed together in 1970 – just him and me. At that point Roland and I had planned to sign a lease for the whole three-quarters of the building, but then he got a permanent job in Canada so I took over the lease. I was literally alone in there; many of the artists had just gone and left just rooms full of junk. Essentially David ran his own part, which ran fairly smoothly, and I had to gradually get in a set of entirely new people. In that first year (1970), I was teaching at Norwich, and I was friendly with a painter called Dick James, so I invited him. He took space at the top floor and we showed together for two years.

David Evison After my first one-man show at Kasmin Limited in 1970, Alan Gouk introduced me to John McLean. He was working in the bedroom of a small flat and I just said to him, 'A space will become available in Stockwell if you're interested.' He came over, had a look and said, 'I'll take it.'

Jennifer Durrant I had the space after my husband and I split up and I had a flat in Camberwell. I was going to Norwich School of Art to teach one day a week at the time, and Dick James – who was teaching there – was working in Stockwell where he had the whole piece under the roof and he wanted to share half of it. I can't remember how much it cost me, but it must have been affordable because I had no money of my own, no family money or anything like that. So, that's how it came about. We partitioned it with polythene but there were only odd occasions when we were there at the same time because of our various part-time teaching commitments.

Katherine Gili I studied for two years on the Advanced Course at St Martin's and Peter Hide, who was one of my tutors, offered me a studio at the end of my second year in June 1973. Anthony Smart, who was a student at the same time as me, was also offered a studio. We joined John Foster and Peter and initially I shared a space with John and Tony, but after a few months I moved into a space of my own. By then I was totally committed to pursuing sculpture and it seemed like a very natural move and a good place to start my career.

Anthony Smart Katherine Gili was by the Pigeon Room, Peter Hide was in his big studio, and John McLean and I were in the roof room, next to him. There was a woman who never turned up who had the first space as you went out to the roof, so we just used that as storage. Upstairs there was Dick James and Jennifer Durrant, and then the art historian John Golding and John McLean were in David Evison's side.

Mark Skilton I initially worked for Tony Smart, who taught me on the degree course at St Martin's from 1973–77; Peter Hide was teaching more on the Advanced Course. I had just built up a rapport with Tony and came to work for him in his studio while I was a student – weekends and things like that – which was great experience for me. Peter saw what I was doing and realised that I would be useful. So when I left St Martin's and was looking for a studio, he was able to offer me one on the proviso that I'd also be able to work for him.

The building

Katherine Gili It was an industrial place with a monolithic brick frontage directly on the street, three storeys high. There were neither frills nor comforts on the inside. I really liked it as a place to work, but – thinking about it now – I imagine some people would find it raw, dark and forbidding; even horrendous. My studio had two small windows quite high up that I could only open with a stick. When it rained, it poured down the back wall because the gutters would overflow. But it didn't bother me; I had a space to work in – what more did I want?! You know, some people ask, 'How does the space affect what you make?' Well, I had a show at the Serpentine in 1977 and that was all made in Stockwell, and I am quite sure that you could not tell what sort of space they were made in.

Jennifer Durrant The building was terribly depressing when I think of it. It was very dark and incredibly cold. In the summer it did get quite hot under the roof if the weather was good, but in the winter the water in the buckets froze over in the studio. Eventually I did have one of those industrial gas heaters, which had a big furnace-like thing on the front. I was so terrified of it that I just turned it on for five-minute blasts. Can you imagine, with all of that polythene, canvas and paper? I don't remember anyone ever coming to inspect the place, but it would have been shut down immediately. Going in, there was a very small front door and you went in and up a metal ramp, stairs, and then round. If they had steel coming in they used to have to take the metal stairs apart – the work they had to do! At that age, in your thirties, you just do these things. A narrow, steep, wooden staircase went up from the first floor to a trap door, which opened up into a vast space under the roof. It was so dark, and then, of course, there was that period sometime in the 70s when you weren't allowed to have electricity – the three-day week – when we covered the windows over so that we could continue to work in the light. At night you always had to have your torch when coming downstairs, out of the building and into the street. There were small terraced houses opposite – very ordinary – and a pub at the end.

John McLean David Evison's half was quite obviously divided architecturally from the very old Victorian part. It was an extremely interesting building. It had a ramp so that horses could be driven up to the first floor – where they were stabled – as well as inclined flooring with a drain for the horse piss to go down.

Paul Tonkin Coming through the door you'd see the scaffolding-pole banister and a metal staircase – very functional, but it also didn't look dangerous at the same time. You kind of felt like it might be, but in fact it was all very solidly made. Then you came up and there was a door through to John McLean's and David Evison's studios. On the right there was another studio at the front of the building, and at the back there was Peter Hide's domain – huge. And behind that there was the roof space, which was just a huge platform. I remember for one private view I got a pianist friend to play, and they hoisted a piano up there. The sculptors were good at that kind of thing. We were all dancing; some of the artists weren't keen on the idea of music, and then those very people were dancing at the end. It was good fun.

The space itself was kind of cavernous and gloomy, the light wasn't great and we had to put gauze over the front windows so that we could hang paintings in between them. Peter's big space had strip lights at the top so it was not great for painting, but it was huge; you could put the biggest paintings you'd done in there and, of course, Peter's massive sculptures. Some of them were vast, towering things, like dinosaurs. There was like a trap door in the ceiling and Jenny Durrant was up there – above Peter – doing vast paintings.

Jennifer Durrant I can remember fixing the polythene partition – we had to do it overhead as well because the space was enormously high. You were under the rafters where this walkway – like a little wooden bridge – went lengthways across where stuff was stored. I don't know why it was there; it had to do with its original use as a brewery.

Neighbours

Peter Hide Lambeth did show a kind of interest in us – and I think even channeled a bit of money to us – but there wasn't a profound influence on the neighbourhood. It was a bit like a bunch of Martians had colonised part of this old building, and there was only the one doorway into it. When we had the openings they were very magnetic for quite a few years; we had lots of drink and tons of people came. It was the place to be, in a way, but that was the art world mainly not the Lambeth folk. They were probably 50 feet away, but they lived in an utterly different world.

Katherine Gili As far as I'm aware, nobody really knew what was going on in the building. There was only one door – not much bigger than a front door – in the side of a brick façade, and the door was kept locked. There were no windows on the ground floor and some on the first floor. It wasn't like other places that needed to involve the community in some way in order to get funding; it was independent, run by Peter Hide and David Evison. Artists went in there to work, they stayed there until whatever hour they wanted to, and left. There were no restrictions on noise.

The studios

David Evison As we were ex-students from St Martin's we were all following a similar kind of path, although some people were a bit more imitative of minimal art than others. And because these large spaces were available, we made large things. Particularly Roelof Louw, from South Africa, who draped his ropes from one end of the building to another. Peter Hide was also starting to use the length of the building to make long steel sculptures. There was another South African guy as well, Roger Fagin, who later on filled a whole room full of railway sleepers.

Gerard Hemsworth For a lot of people, when they leave art school, they find it quite difficult to start operating in a studio because there's no structure and sometimes it's quite difficult to make work. There's not a canteen or a library that you can go to; you just sit there or you go home. Stockwell, in that respect, was quite supportive because in those moments where nothing really was happening for you, you could go and chat to somebody else who might feel the same. I think it takes quite some time for people to develop a studio practice. Whilst I was a student I worked as an assistant for both Phillip King and Bill Tucker; I was quite good at making things, so they employed me. I was quite taken aback at how rigorous they were with timing – particularly Phillip, who started early in the morning and worked right the way through.

When I was first at Stockwell I had no teaching; I was on the dole. Then I got a job in the British Museum making copies of their sculptures, which of course meant that I was only getting to the studio in the evening. I suppose it was like a slice of reality to have to work five days a week and then be at the studio on evenings and weekends. The following year I got two days a week teaching and I could spend a lot more time in the studio.

David Evison I worked in wood and cheap materials. There were some benches in the building that could be sawed up to make sculpture, and I used those. I worked in wood because I had no money; I couldn't afford a welder but I could afford a saw and a hammer. A lot happened in that first year; Tony Caro brought John Kasmin round and he bought a piece from me and one or two others. He was interested in us and wanted to show us in a group exhibition in Dusseldorf, it must have been after the Stockwell show in 1968. When Kasmin started to support me, I was able to buy more equipment.

Peter Hide Initially the idea was to find somewhere in which we could work together and pool our money for tools, welding equipment and oxyacetylene, that sort of thing. We hadn't thought about it in specific terms of a space, we just thought about the economies of scale because we couldn't afford the equipment on our own. The Port of

London was gone as a proper port and the old buildings were falling vacant all over the city. People didn't know what to do with them – they were an embarrassment, I suppose, to councils. Then with this boom in art education and all these students leaving it made sense for the building to be used – it was a changing demographic.

Katherine Gili Actually – and surprisingly – in those days all one needed was three pieces of equipment: a grinder, a welder and oxyacetylene cutting gear. I had my own equipment but we did help each other with some practical things. John Foster helped me on a couple of occasions with welding and drilling.

The sculpture studios were on the first floor of the building, with a double flight of stairs up from ground level and a single doorway opening to the street. In order to get oxygen and acetylene gas bottles to the studios we had to pull them up the stairs with ropes. They were very heavy, especially the acetylene. When we needed to buy scrap steel we would club together to hire a three-ton flat-bed truck to go to the scrapyard. We would each pick the pieces we wanted – angle iron, girders, plate and bars – out of the huge piles of scrap, and then cranes with magnets lifted the steel up to put on our lorry.

Once back at the Depot it was a question of getting all this steel upstairs and inside. At the back and to the side of the building there was an ambulance yard, which gave us access to the flat roof, which was also used for exhibiting sculpture. The steel had to be brought on to the roof with a small crane jib, fixed to the side of the building, and a manual chain block hoist, so we had to pull on a chain to lift the steel from the ground to the roof deck. It was then taken on trollies across the length of the roof into the studios, which in my case meant taking it through Peter's studio and down the corridor. The whole process could take two or three days. When John Foster left, I took over driving the trucks because at that time neither Tony Smart nor Peter Hide could drive.

John McLean I got this much bigger studio which, whilst an increase in scale, was technically just as messy from throwing paint around. When I worked in my flat I would put polythene over the floor and about one foot up the side of the walls because it was that messy. So my approach to painting didn't change, I could just do more.

Quite a few people would have been using squeegees, working on the floor. I made one that was five or six foot across – it had cross-bracing so it could push great amounts. The canvas wasn't on a stretcher, it was stapled to a large board which I think was Kasmin's old flooring that he had specially used for showing Tony Caro's *Prairie* (1967). He managed to get Evison to store it for him and I started pirating it. The paint would go right through the canvas and puddle, and those puddles would come back onto the surface because the canvas was only nine ounces – it was like painting on scaled-up tissue paper.

David Evison In our first year we were visited by Peter Sedgely and Bridget Riley; they wanted to see what a group studio situation was like. They explained that they were about to set up this kind of space in St Katharine Docks. I don't know if they learned anything from us – I doubt it – but I had a good friend who took on a space there, Alan Green – a good painter. He taught me when I was at Leeds College of Art and I visited him in his studio a few times – it was really well organised. They set up this organisation called SPACE and it was like a little business, properly run with decent toilets and things, while ours was just grotty.

John McLean Stockwell Depot was one of the first – if not the first – big industrial buildings to be taken over in London. I think it pre-dated the artists getting hold of St Katharine Docks and this was acknowledged in the art bureaucracy – for years we got a grant to put on an annual exhibition.

Exhibitions at Stockwell Depot

Peter Hide The first exhibition was not funded by the Arts Council, but we did have a catalogue introduction written by Michael Compton of the Tate Gallery. Roland Brener was a great networker. The artists who showed were Alan Barkley, Roland Brener, David Evison, Roger Fagin, John Fowler, Gerard Hemsworth, Roelof Louw and myself. The exhibitions were like the climax of the year. The first group only showed together twice, and then after that quite a lot of the initial group drifted away.

David Evison The first show was a local event for the 'in' people who came up from St Martin's; the second was the one Nigel Greenwood put together and it was mobbed – loads of people came. Everyone was complaining about having to come south of the river and the fact that the Depot was kind of dank and dirty – all these kinds of things – rather than about the art. We got newspaper reviews and I seem to remember getting bad reviews, but I wasn't interested – I think I threw them away. Someone wrote, 'Sometimes it seems like Zadkine rides again.' After that I got my own gallery and one or two other group exhibition venues. By this time I had started to fight with Peter Hide, although I shouldn't put it like that because we never came to blows.

Katherine Gili Everyone who worked there did not necessarily take part in the annual shows regularly except Peter Hide, John McLean, Tony Smart and myself from 1974. Painters from outside were included from 1975 and only a few showed regularly thereafter. There was very little socialising as such. We all had to earn a living from various part-time jobs which meant that we were not always in the building together on the same days. So the annual shows were the main opportunity to see what each of us had done and this was when serious discussions took place.

John McLean I think that Alan Gouk and Peter Hide probably discussed expanding the Depot exhibitions to include other artists in a natural, ordinary way, over a pint together. I didn't take any interest in that – I was a willing participant, but I never wanted to introduce any more people into the exhibitions. I think that I just thought of it as somewhere we showed once a year, rather than as a vehicle for promotion. I've always been a bit slow on that front.

Alan Gouk In the summer of 1974 we went to the Spaniards Inn after an exhibition of Caro's and Peter Hide proposed to Geoff Rigden and I that we join forces and have a joint exhibition of painting and sculpture. The painting committee – if you like – was me, Fred Pollock and Geoff; then Paul Tonkin in 1976.

The painters and sculptors who worked in The Annexe were not so central to Peter's plans – outside his domain, as it were. John McLean ended up in the shows although he wouldn't take part in the hang; we would come in to do the selection and John would already have hung his pictures in the prime spot – the first room – which was the only room that had any natural light. I suppose that he felt entitled, since his studio was in the Depot, whereas the rest of us were interlopers, as it were. John was able to exert quite an influence because John Golding – also with a studio in The Annexe – was one of the grey eminences on the Arts Council committee. Golding never took part, or rather, he was never asked. Whilst it did get Arts Council patronage on a small scale for the catalogue, invites and things, it was basically seen as an independent venture – independent of Caro, independent of everything – but we had to get some money to pay for expenses and things.

John McLean Nobody thought to ask John Golding to take part in the shows. He was ten years older and a little bit apart from everybody else, not – so to speak – one of the lads. There was only one occasion when he came and had a pint in the local pub; I had a show approaching and I was desperate to do more work than I could manage in my studio, so I used his whilst he was away as well as my own. When he came back I gave him the rent but he demurred and instead said, 'We'll all go for a drink with the rent money.' That's the only occasion that the others and I went to the local pub with him.

Paul Tonkin I was in the shows from 1976–78 with Fred Pollock, Douglas Abercrombie and Alan Gouk. We would look in threes at the fourth artist's work and select paintings from what they had brought along; it was quite democratic in that way.

Maybe it was a bit arrogant of us, but we didn't see any reason to include anyone else until the last exhibition in 1979 when it was decided to broaden the whole show out. I really enjoyed the way we hung the shows; it seemed to me that the works were bouncing off each other, almost feeding off each other. There was some common feeling there but it's hard to explain what it was.

Katherine Gili From a personal viewpoint the exhibitions were an opportunity to step back from what you had made and see it freshly in a clear exhibition space, as well as to see it alongside others' work. The sculptural ideas that were seen formed the basis for discussion. Questions were raised, not about technique or about craft but about how sculpture could achieve and express greater physicality, and each sculptor went away and looked for their own answers. The work changed and developed every year, and as the shows were open to the public they also became an important part of the art scene. A lot of people took notice; they were reviewed in *Artscribe* as well as other magazines and periodicals, and became part of the general debate.

Alan Gouk The openings were very well attended by art-world people, like Anthony Reynolds, who then opened up a gallery of his own. Obviously they didn't think much of it because I felt it got little coverage in the magazines – and what there was, was negative. And then, of course, there was the relationship with Caro. He tried to keep it within his orbit of influence – within his empire.

John McLean I remember once, when Peter Hide was the main organiser of one of the Stockwell shows, he gave everyone a task and asked me to be the one to see that it was well reviewed. I went off to *Studio International* where the editorship had just been taken over by Richard Cork. I went to the office to meet him and said, 'I hope you're going to review this', and he just said, 'No'. I looked at him, turned on my heel and walked out – I didn't know what to say.

Anthony Caro

Peter Hide As students we were all, I guess, brought up under the influence of Anthony Caro. Most of us had – at one stage or another – been working out of his work pretty closely. I think that all of us wanted to, in varying degrees, escape from that influence.

Alan Gouk Peter Hide and I were trying to consolidate and hold together a concept, an idea of the value of a shared ethos, shared ambitions and shared criticisms; the sort of things that are a direct continuation of the sculpture Forums at St Martin's and the critiques we gave of one another's work. In a sense, the Forums were a direct product of Caro's teaching method. There was one occasion when we all went to a panel discussion with, I think, people like Richard Cork, Lynne Cooke and Caroline Tisdall. There must have been a certain amount of rowdiness and maybe a bit of heckling. One of the panel got up and said, 'Mr Caro, I wonder if you could keep your coterie in better control', or something similar. We were suffering from both ends; we were seen as Caro's gang – but very much subservient – and also as these bolshie people. It didn't get us anywhere.

Anthony Smart I would say that it was the publicity of the Depot that brought students into St Martin's in the early 1970s. Whereas previously it had been about Caro, suddenly it was about these young, rebel types.

Mark Skilton When I went to work in Dundee in 1980 for my first teaching job, everyone there knew about Stockwell Depot. Although there was a lot of respect and awe for the place, they also knew it as a bit of a beast to be slain. Certainly the sculpture was often approached with aggression in the studio – we'd get these big sheets in and just hack them to pieces – but ultimately it was the sensitivity of the work that gave it any quality.

Alan Gouk In 'Steel Sculpture Part II' (2014) I describe how, in 1978, Peter Hide got hold of these big, thick, pastry-like rolled steel ends. Caro had used these some years before but Peter stacked them up vertically into these masses, for example in *Left Arm Chinaman* (1979; p.143). Tony Smart had already made some sculptures by massing plates together in his Tamarind series of 1977 (p.123). 'Corporeality' and 'physicality' were becoming the watchwords, and in 1978 Kathy's sculptures became more condensed and object-like as well.

Collective identity

Gerard Hemsworth Initially our collective need for Stockwell Depot was studio space. It's a curious time in an artist's life when they first leave art school. You do a lot of growing up; trying to find out what is important for you; what is the consequence of your education. Stockwell Depot developed an agenda – which was not interesting for me – derived from a narrow view of abstract art and the teaching of Anthony Caro.

Peter Hide At the beginning, there were people who were nearer the conceptual approach – like Roelof Louw and Gerard Hemsworth – and then there were people who were more conservatively modernist like David Evison, John Fowler and myself. So there was a spectrum of artists at Stockwell which also reflected the spectrum at St Martin's.

Katherine Gili There was – amongst everyone who worked at the Depot – a commitment and a shared aim to improve the quality of their work, but each artist worked separately towards it. In my mind, that on its own does not constitute a community. I am not sure that the studios could be considered as communal; the place was more fragmented than that, especially when you think that most of us did not work there for very long. Stockwell Depot did, however, represent an attitude towards the making of sculpture. To put it simply, we all worked in steel and made free-standing, non-referential, sculpture: that was our common ground, our position. We were not alone in this – other people were making steel sculpture elsewhere – but it was the shows that gave it a focus for the four of us in particular. I know that some people saw Stockwell as representing something narrow, but I disagree. If you focus on something particular it doesn't make it narrow, in fact the more one concentrates on something the more things open up and the more there is to find.

Painters and sculptors

Mark Skilton I suppose the sculpture that I identified most with was that by Tony Smart, we just seemed to have a common kind of feel about what we wanted sculpture to be. Tony – who was living in Yorkshire at the time – would come down and stay with Geoff Hollow and me and we would all talk about sculpture and painting. Geoff really got me into trying to understand painting. It was that sort of dialogue – together with what was happening at St Martin's – that was a big influence.

John McLean I have always been intrigued by sculpture, I enjoy looking at it. I must have taken in an awful lot whilst I was there, but the painter who really impressed me was Jenny Durrant. I didn't at the time get anything from it – although I admired what she did – but I think I would have to acknowledge now that my use of collage has quite a lot to do with her successful use of the medium. Jenny did once say that she thought my work had developed the way it did because all my friends were sculptors rather than painters. I think there may be a grain of truth there, but also a great deal of exaggeration.

Paul Tonkin I guess it might be to do with the nature of the work, but the sculptors were very passionate about their beliefs and had very strong opinions. I'm generalising of course, but they invest a lot of hard physical work in what they do whereas painting is a bit more fluid and flexible somehow. Painters generally seem to have a different way of discussing or looking at each other's work – they are a bit more laid back.

Clement Greenberg and Abstract Expressionism

John McLean When Clement Greenberg visited I associated it utterly with Anthony Caro encouraging him to come. I remember David Evison reminiscing about an early visit in 1968 when Greenberg kicked a circular sculpture – I think it was by Roelof Louw. As he kicked (well, tapped it anyway, dismissively with his foot) he said, 'An American would have opened the circle up.' But Greenberg didn't hold any sway. We were all independent.

Gerard Hemsworth On that day in 1968 when Greenberg came, I couldn't be there because I was teaching, but I did set up some work in my studio with the hope that he would go in. Some time later I asked David Annesley whether he went in and how much time he spent there. He sort of hummed and hawed so I said, 'Tell me exactly how much time he spent', and he said, 'Well, he spent as much time as it takes to walk into the studio and walk out again.' I said, 'Oh right,' and Annesley said, 'Yeah, he's got a trained eye' – I thought, 'Fuck off!' I don't know whether that confirmed my feelings about where I wanted to align myself (I mean, what would have happened if Greenberg liked the work?) but he definitely was fairly dismissive about what I was doing and that somehow put me into another camp. So I'm sort of grateful to him for that.

Jennifer Durrant I went to the US with David Evison and Alan Gouk in 1972; David had sold a sculpture to a collector in the Boston area, a member of the Cabot family. I didn't know anything about contemporary American art when I was at Brighton Art College, then when I was at the Slade I had just started to experience non-figurative painting. So the history of American Expressionism, Abstract Expressionism and, well, the Europeans going to America – that was all new to me. The three of us went to Greenberg's New York apartment. A discussion took place about Monet, and afterwards David and Alan wouldn't speak to me in the lift and I assumed that was because I had perhaps shown my ignorance – I thought they were embarrassed. You can imagine how arrogant they were, these young men.

When Greenberg visited Stockwell to see the sculptors he asked who else was working in the building, and possibly John said, 'Well, there's Jenny upstairs.' Whether Greenberg remembered me from that trip to New York, I don't know, but he made me show him absolutely everything and was there for ages. At one point he said – which was very misogynist, I suppose – 'Oh, shut up woman, I don't want to hear what you've got to say, I just want to look.' I suppose with my background and how I was then, I was too apologetic I expect.

Paul Tonkin I think that in retrospect, what Fred Pollock, Douglas Abercrombie, Alan Gouk and I had in common was that we were greatly influenced by north-American post-painterly abstraction, as it was known. Yet at the same time we tried to find a way around that by looking at paintings by the previous generation – including Hans Hofmann, Clyfford Still and Adolph Gottlieb – as well as others like Jack Bush and of course the old masters, who I was just discovering in the National Gallery. We were trying to avoid becoming transatlantic, as we saw it, and also wanting to reintroduce a painterly approach to our work.

Alan Gouk One of the grounds for the antagonism towards us was that we were the only ones who were positive about the American connection, where so many other English painters were cynical. There was also clearly some resentment about the Greenberg connection – he was getting a lot of criticism from all quarters of the British art-critical scene. From our point of view, we were being drawn back to places that we were trying to leave behind; we were being put in a bag marked 'Caroesque' whilst also being put through hoops by Caro himself through his advocacy of Clement Greenberg – Greenberg didn't even want to go see our work, but Caro insisted. We were being pulled constantly in the direction of emulating the painting from New York, while our actual work was moving in the opposite direction – or trying to, in most cases.

Mark Skilton Greenberg had a look at everyone's work, including mine. He did pick up on details of what I was doing but, well, they were pretty crazy sculptures. They were quite dense – information-dense as well as material-dense. We were struggling with pictoriality and how to expand it without actually giving up the pictorial way of working. You can imagine how troublesome that would be. In comparison, Peter Hide was making very clear things with a clear outline which Greenberg related to instantly – it fitted into his ideas about what sculpture could be. I did, however, get a positive vibe from him. He sensed that I was a young sculptor at the time and had some promise, which was in a way reassuring.

Paul Tonkin When I was at art school in 1971 or 72, I got a copy of Greenberg's *Art and Culture* (1961). I was walking down a corridor with it and another guy, in the year above me, walked past and said, 'Your bible.' And I'd never even looked at it before, you know? If you mentioned the name Greenberg – or any of the painters he promoted – you were seen as an idoliser, a 'Greenbergite'. We were young and impressionable, of course, but we weren't members of a cult. Greenberg exposed much contemporary art as kitsch and he upset a lot of vested interests. I felt that there were some really obnoxious people who loathed him and tried to make out that he was a tool of the CIA, and all that kind of shit. Okay it did emerge that the CIA – well, the Americans – were funding him, but so what? It's just like the British Council.

Endgames

Anthony Smart From 1973 Stockwell Depot, with its studios and exhibitions, was for me the hub of the major events in abstract sculpture making. One by one the notion of ideas and design and other conceptual prescriptions gradually gave way to a more direct format of working with the material – steel. The vision was to examine the things that could be part of abstract sculpture that would not be dependent on other disciplines such as painting and architecture. What the pieces looked like and what determined their meaning became the thing to be invented directly with the material.

Retrospectively, that generation of sculptors turned the practice of previous generations into what I now term 'freestyle sculpture'. For me, that second period (1973–82) at Stockwell Depot was the trigger for everything else to come; it put the demands on to the work that introduced the full variety of sculptural language that we have today, rather than the various hybrids we previously settled for as answers to more singular questions.

Alan Gouk Probably the most significant year of all for Stockwell was 1979; they had some final, big discussions and decided that the bulky, corporeal sculpture – as they called it – was going nowhere. Glynn Williams was part of that, but then there was a falling out with him too. It is all tied in with developments with the sculpture course at St Martin's in its latter years – it's all linked.

Mark Skilton There was some unhappiness with the way that pictorial sculpture had settled into this style, which everyone was copying – it seemed almost inevitable. In trying to break from that style I went for density, but then we started using thicker and thicker bits of plate which turned out to be a red herring, and it sort of took over. I think that it became obvious during the 1979 show that we had taken it as far as we could. Bob Persey was working with five-inch plate and I was working with two and three-inch plate – there was nowhere else that you could go with that, it had reached its logical conclusion but there were no ideas on the table about how to move forward. This all coincided – more or less – with Peter Hide going to Canada; he carried on working in heavy, chunky steel but he placed one flat plane against another with distinct outlines, and almost some kind of recognisable image. Pretty soon after that there was the 'Lion Project' at St Martin's where we looked at this Greek lion sculpture and tried to analyse it and make something from it in metal. The idea just had legs; immediately we started working in a different way because the lion itself was a three-dimensional sculpture, so we sensed the possibilities. For decades, really, we were unaware of the significance of it. At the time we sensed that it was new and the work had a different kind of feel – a vitality of its own – but we couldn't put into words what that was.

Alan Gouk By 1979 the various projects, including 'From the Body' and 'Paperwork', had started with the students at St Martin's. Tony Smart and Kathy Gili continued to make these abstract or planar-type sculptures, but you can see the changes beginning to take place in the sculptures they showed in the 1979 show. Kathy didn't make a lion, but some of the students started working from the lion first. Tony started a project working from an Ionian lion in the British Museum with students on the Foundation course at St Martin's, which Tim Scott then picked up on. The first thing Tim did on becoming Head of Sculpture at St Martin's in 1979 was to acquire a cast of the lion. I had introduced the model into the projects on the Advanced Course the previous year, although nothing like the way the model had served in the past.

Paul Tonkin The *Hayward Annual 1980* was, I think, a landmark show, but I would say that, wouldn't I? Frank Bowling was in that show, and he's a damn good painter, as well as some of us from Stockwell. The exhibition got a mention in some newspapers, but it all seemed to fall flat because suddenly there was a big exhibition at the Royal Academy at exactly the same time called *A New Spirit in Painting*. The Royal Academy show had huge, figurative, painterly paintings; Georg Baselitz was one of them – his gimmick was doing things upside down – and there was someone else whose gimmick was using broken crockery. I thought that those paintings were awful and the work in the *Hayward Annual* was much more interesting, but that was the fashion. Suddenly abstract painting had become very unfashionable.

Alan Gouk I remember the exhibition, *Sculpture from Stockwell Depot*, at the Sainsbury Centre in 1982. It's a big building – like a hangar – designed by Norman Foster; the end wall is completely in glass with a huge, kind of Venetian blind operated mechanically. It was a sunny evening and as the Venetian blind went up you could see, basking on the green lawn, this big, glossy, bronze Henry Moore sculpture. Next to it, the figure sculptures by Tony Smart and Kathy Gili looked like they were from a different planet. Caro was there at the opening – when he saw Tony and Kathy's pieces he said, 'Oh, this is where I came in', but they said, 'No it isn't. You didn't deal with it in any intense depth.'

Mark Skilton I think the aggressive persona attributed to Stockwell sculpture got exaggerated out of all proportion. It was there, but those that wanted to see the downfall of steel sculpture and the Depot would exaggerate the nature of that aggression. It was seen as something extremely negative and exclusive, which it wasn't. It wasn't that anyone wanted to exclude other sculptors from the Depot or from making steel sculpture. It was just that a high standard had to be maintained.

Katherine Gili The thing is – and this is entirely natural – the more that one develops, the more that common ground becomes stretched and the less useful discussion becomes. That is why the shows came to an end, but the fact is the artists carried on and that is also part of the legacy.

A pamphlet containing full transcripts of these interviews has been printed to coincide with the exhibition *Stockwell Depot 1967–79* at the University of Greenwich Galleries, London, 2015.

The Concerns of Emerging Sculptors

Roland Brener, 1969

At this time, for the sculptor to develop a critical attitude not only towards the sculpture being produced, but the context in which it is made and exhibited, is necessary.

As it exists now, when considered as a specialised activity relating to a spectrum of other activities, sculpture is of trivial consequence: it does not change or influence the way people live, disturb their prejudices, or have as much potential in challenging their perception as many other visual media.

When considered as a pure, creative form – which is its own justification – sculpture nevertheless has many anomalies, which could do with some criticism. If current attitudes are indicative of future policy it seems unlikely that sculpture will become a permanent feature of our environment, unless as a whimsical decorative extension to architecture. That is, as it exists now. It is primarily through exhibitions that the sculptor and public relate. Unfortunately the criteria on which this relationship is based are arbitrary to the content of the work and meaningless outside the given situation. The accepted methods of showing sculpture – in galleries, museums and temporary exhibitions – reinforce the general image of the sculptor as a minor transitory performer. Lack of empathy between artist and viewer arises because they do not communicate on a basis of equality. In most exhibitions the work exists on a par with ritualistic or fetishist objects, with the viewer in the denigrated role of one who has come to pay homage, a situation obviously precluding any meaningful dialogue. At the same time, in defence of the artist, the onus is on the viewer to experience the work from the standpoint that the artist assumes. The effort not to make judgements based on familiarity or preconditioned responses seems to be more than most people are prepared to attempt.

It is made quite apparent that the prevailing system will not change radically by the complacency of artists already integrated into the existing commercial structure, and the inability of authoritative bodies to anticipate change (for example, the new 'progressive administration of the Institute of Contemporary Art, London and the opening of the Hayward Gallery, London, a totally unimaginative and inflexible exhibition space). The inane standard of British art criticism, orientated more towards verbal stylistic conventions than visual or social analytical thought, is an essential contributory factor to the perpetuation of outdated standards.

That sculpture is produced seriously at all is due to a minority interest and sponsorship with which the sculptor must make some form of compromise. As an artist, it would be absurd to adopt a moralistic attitude towards those artists who have received a degree of public recognition, and work within the existing structure. The argument for a system based on different criteria can be seen as one of expedience rather than idealism, for the cost of being a sculptor in England ensures that dependence on a moneyed elite of patrons will remain constant. However, a situation free from pressures to conform is an abstract concept. Freedom exists when one recognises the nature of the pressures and one's own response to them. In other words it exists presuming the artist is aware of his impotent social and ethical position or the basic duality of his values.

If developing sculptors feel that the commercial system operating now cannot absorb them, they must attempt to bypass what they see as an exclusive situation. Dealers' galleries have neither the space nor the financial means to show young sculptors who cannot be considered a good investment, especially if the sculpture is too large to be accommodated by most private buyers. If the galleries are unable to provide an outlet, the sculptor is dependent – for the privilege of showing his work – on selections made by exhibition committees and other organisers, whose motives and knowledge are often more than suspect.

For those on the outside, the 'art establishment' seems conspiratorial and impregnable. For those on the inside it seems mythical – it does not exist, except possibly with reference to others. The passive attitude of the established sculptors are not to be blamed; they have achieved what they need – a secure situation conducive to the making of their work. The needs of the emerging sculptors are no different, but in order to achieve that degree of security they must reject the precedents created for them.

Anthony Caro infused dynamic potential into British sculpture, and this was to a limited degree exploited by the New Generation sculptors. The initial excitement felt at the first New Generation exhibition has faded, despite the continuing efforts of the Whitechapel Art Gallery, London, to contrive annual experiences of a similar nature. In the exhibition of 1965 the salient common factor was the apparent emancipation from traditional conceptual inhibitions. That exhibition resulted in a widespread recognition and acceptance of the sculptors, and their subsequent work has perhaps suffered as a result. They have, for the most part, lapsed into a form of sculptural rhetoric, but perhaps it is reasonable for the artist to make one bold statement that he then consolidates and refines until it ceases to elicit a positive response? Art can evolve only to a predictable point within an established idiom and the gallery-type situation is itself restrictive enough to limit sculptural possibilities. The New Generation sculptors accepted this limitation and have not up until now questioned or analysed their mode of exposition. The (theoretical) concern with 'realness' and 'openness' – the attempt to free sculpture from a descriptive function and associative connotations – fails if the work relies for its success on the specialised environment made for it. The contrived social and environmental situation in which it works best is its own contradiction.

So if it were possible to make generalisations about the concerns of emerging sculptors, their problems could be defined in opposing ways:

(a) They are working from a conceptual basis as contributors to a theoretical continuum dealing with accepted sculptural problems.

(b) They are paradoxically forced into a radical position in their quest for recognition and security.

At Stockwell Depot I am participating with seven other sculptors in a situation that could be regarded as an experiment in extending personal criteria to cover the full cycle of involvement, from concept and raw material to exposition and feedback. The Depot is a large (17,000 square foot), redundant brewery that serves as a workspace and exhibition area. The first exhibition held there during May 1968 received an unexpectedly forthright response, not only from those with an immediate interest but also from a broad, cultural cross-section of people. The reason for this was the openness of the situation: the sculptors involved were generally available for information and comment, and the building provides varied spaces that have a positive character and atmosphere. The work itself could be criticised for the degree to which it interacted or did not interact with the space, and for the tentative or gestural quality of much of it. This could be a result of the short time we had then occupied the building and the difficulties in relating – or even deciding – the degree to which we should relate to each other. We do not share a common style and exist as a group only in that we are all in one place at one time. Whether or not any work of importance will ever be made or shown at Stockwell remains to be seen. The potential in the situation exists because the artists themselves are solely responsible for its success or failure.

First published in *Studio International*, vol.177, no.907, January 1969, p.25.

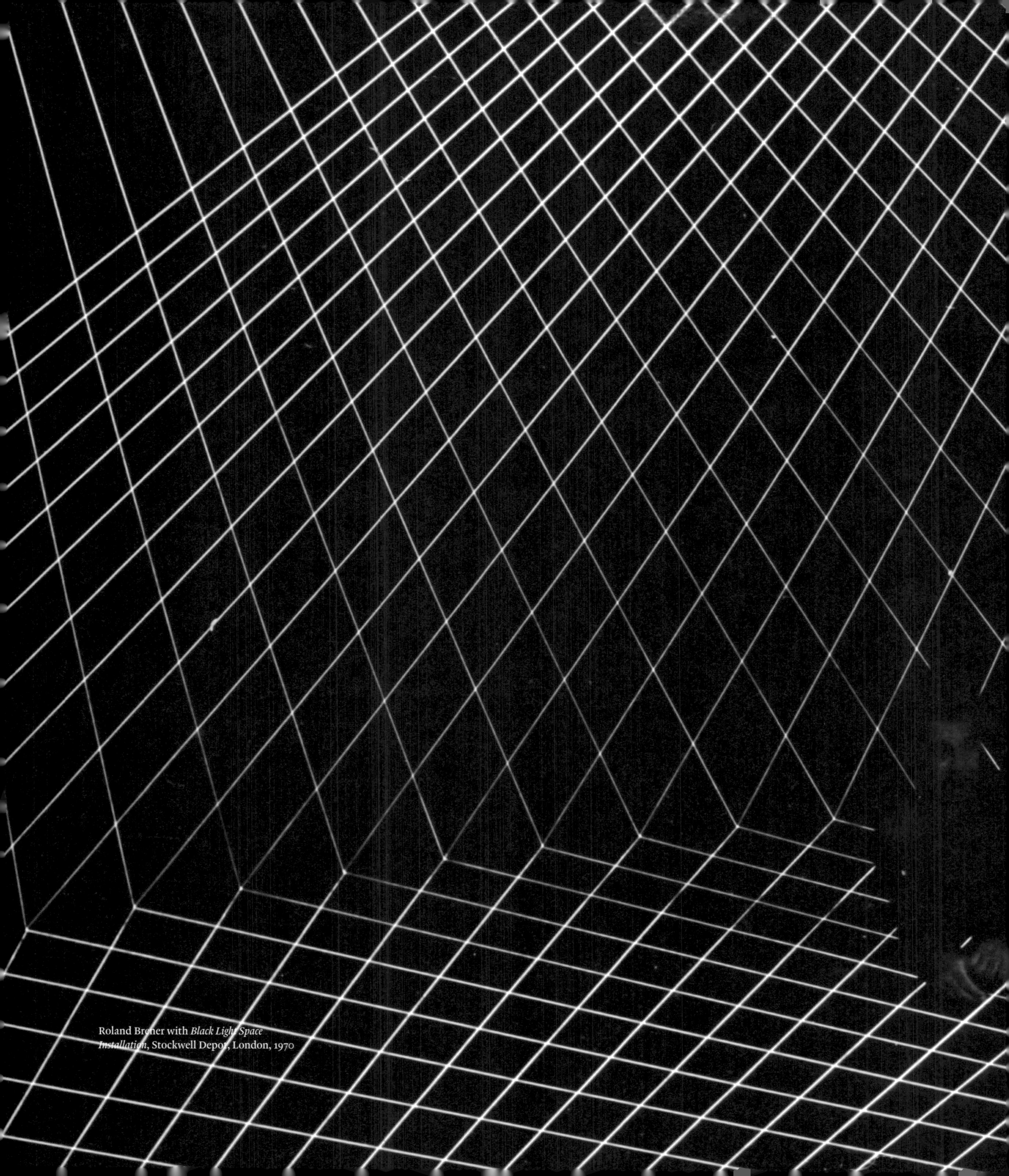

Roland Brener with *Black Light Space Installation*, Stockwell Depot, London, 1970

Biographies

* **Studied sculpture at St Martin's School of Art, London.**

Douglas Abercrombie

Born 1934, Glasgow, UK.
Lives and works in London and Scotland, UK.
Exhibited at Stockwell Depot 1978–79.

Selected exhibitions:
1958 57 Gallery, Edinburgh, UK. **1959** Danish Institute, Edinburgh, UK. **1961** Citizens Theatre, Glasgow, UK. **1963** Thames Gallery, Windsor, UK. **1969** Steyer Gallery, Lippstadt, Germany. **1977** *Studio Exhibition*, Bombay Wharf, London, UK. **1977** *British Painting 1952–1977*, Royal Academy of Arts, London, UK. **1977** *Four Abstract Artists*, Fruitmarket Gallery, Edinburgh, UK. **1979** *Two from Stockwell*, City Art Gallery, Leeds, UK. **1980** *The New Generation: A Curator's Choice*, André Emmerich Gallery, New York, NY, US. **1982** *Summer Show 2*, Serpentine Gallery, London, UK. **2005** *Mainstream Abstract Painting from the Seventies*, Poussin Gallery, London, UK. **2008** *A Painting Retrospective*, Poussin Gallery, London, UK. **2012** *Douglas Abercrombie: New Paintings; Peter Hide: New Sculptures*, Poussin Gallery, London, UK.

Alan Barkley*

Born 1944, Belleville, Canada.
Lives and works in Old Lyme, CT, US.
Studio at Stockwell Depot 1968–70.
Exhibited at Stockwell Depot 1968–69.

Selected exhibitions:
1970 *Stockwell Depot: Eight English Sculptors from London*, Kunstnernes Hus, Oslo, Norway and Konsthallen, Gothenburg, Sweden. **1971** *Art Spectrum North*, Manchester City Art Gallery, Manchester, UK. **1978** *Passage*, Southern Alberta Art Gallery, Lethbridge, Canada. **1980** Art Gallery of Ontario, Toronto, Canada. **1982** Eyelevel Gallery, Halifax, Canada.

Stephenie Bergman

Born 1946, London, UK.
Lives and works in Ollioules, France and Taroudant, Morocco.
Exhibited at Stockwell Depot 1975.

Selected exhibitions:
1974 Garage Art Ltd, London, UK. **1975** *Stephenie Bergman and Nicholas Pope*, Southampton City Art Gallery, Southampton, UK. **1976** *John Moores Exhibition*, Walker Art Gallery, Liverpool, UK. **1977** Kettle's Yard, Cambridge, UK. **1977** *British Painting 1952–1977*, Royal Academy of Arts, London, UK. **1979** *Style in the Seventies*, Arnolfini Gallery, Bristol, UK. **1981** XIème Biennale de Jeunes, Musée de l'Art Moderne, Paris, France. **1983** *Whitechapel Open*, Whitechapel Art Gallery, London, UK. **1984** Crafts Council Gallery, London, UK. **1986** Nigel Greenwood, London, UK. **1987** *Vessel*, Serpentine Gallery, London, UK. **1993** *The Raw and the Cooked: New Work in Clay in Britain*, Barbican Art Gallery, London, UK. **1998** *Barely Made*, Norwich School of Art Gallery, Norwich, UK. **2000** *Opening Exhibition*, David Gill Galleries, London, UK. **2006** *Artist's House*, New Art Centre, Wiltshire, UK. **2011** Marsden Woo Gallery, London, UK.

Roland Brener*

Born 1942, Johannesburg, South Africa.
Died 2006, Victoria, Canada.
Studio at Stockwell Depot 1967–72.
Exhibited at Stockwell Depot 1968–70.

Selected exhibitions:
1967 Kasmin Limited, London, UK. **1968** Prospect 68, Kunsthalle Düsseldorf, Dusseldorf, Germany. **1969** *New Sculpture 1969*, Arts Council touring exhibition, UK. **1970** Nigel Greenwood Gallery, London, UK. **1970** *Stockwell Depot: Eight English Sculptors from London*, Kunstnernes Hus, Oslo, Norway and Konsthallen, Gothenburg, Sweden. **1970** *British Sculpture Out of the Sixties*, Institute of Contemporary Art, London, UK. **1970** *Recent Art in Britain*, Leeds City Art Gallery, Leeds, UK. **1971** Santa Barbara Museum of Art, Santa Barbara, CA, US. **1973** Museum of Art, Iowa City, IA, US. **1974** Vancouver Art Gallery, Vancouver, Canada. **1978** Art Gallery of Greater Victoria, Victoria, Canada. **1980** *Pluralities/1980/Pluralities*, National Gallery of Canada, Ottawa, Canada. **1982** *Mise en Scène*, Vancouver Art Gallery, Vancouver, Canada. **1983** Edmonton Art Gallery, Edmonton, Canada. **1986** *Art in Victoria*, Victoria Art Gallery, Victoria, Canada. **1987** São Paolo Biennale, São Paolo, Brazil. **1991** *Site Memory*, Cleveland Center for Contemporary Art, Cleveland, OH, US. **1994** *Modern Metal*, London Regional Art Gallery, London, UK. **1997** *Discoveries in Digital Design*, Portland Institute for Contemporary Art, Portland, OR, US. **2000** Deitch Projects, New York, NY, US. **2005** *30 Years in Victoria: Roland Brener and Mowry Baden*, Art Gallery of Greater Victoria, Victoria, Canada. **2010** *Art at Work: Corporate Collecting Practices Today*, Art Gallery of Mississauga, Mississauga, Canada.

Shirley Cameron*

Born 1944, Oxford, UK.
Lives and works in Sheffield, UK.
Studio at Stockwell Depot 1967–68.

Selected exhibitions:
1964 *Young Ideas*, Saint Martin's Gallery, London, UK. **1965** *Young Contemporaries*, FBA Gallery, London, UK. **1967** *New Directions*, Camden Arts Centre, London, UK. **1967** *British Sculpture and Painting*, Whitechapel Art Gallery, London, UK. **1968** *Sculpture in the City*, City of London Festival, London, UK. **1972** *Squares of Experience*, Serpentine Gallery, London, UK. **1973** *User Boxes*, Angela Flowers Gallery, London, UK. **1973** *Naming Our Vision*, Serpentine Gallery, London and Walker Art Gallery, Liverpool, UK. **1974** *Landscapes and Living Spaces*, International Performance Festival, Birmingham, UK. **1975** Performances in *Les Six Jours de la Peinture*, Marseille, France. **1977** *The 100 Holes*, Walker Art Gallery, Liverpool, UK. **1989** Mappin Art Gallery, Sheffield, UK. **1991** *Silver and Gold*, Tate Gallery, London, UK. **1994** *Cake Face*, Spacex Gallery, Exeter, UK. **2002** *Rooms within Rooms*, Bolsover Castle, Bolsover, UK. **2006** Lewis Glucksman Gallery, Cork, Ireland. **2011** *United Enemies: The Problem of Sculpture in Britain in the 1960s and 1970s*, Henry Moore Institute, Leeds, UK. **2013** *re.act.feminism*, Akademie der Künste, Berlin, Germany.

Jeff Dellow

Born 1949, Newcastle upon Tyne, UK.
Lives and works in London, UK.
Exhibited at Stockwell Depot 1979.

Selected exhibitions:
1979 *Open Attitudes*, Museum of Modern Art, Oxford, UK. **1980** *Seven Painters*, Kettle's Yard, Cambridge, UK. **1980** *Hayward Annual*, Hayward Gallery, London, UK. **1983** *Whitechapel Open*, Whitechapel Art Gallery, London, UK. **1984** *100 Artists*, The Showroom Gallery, London, UK. **1987** Castlefield Gallery, Manchester, UK. **1988** *Two Painters: Jeffrey Dellow and George Percy*, Woodlands Gallery, London, UK. **1989** *John Moores Exhibition*, Walker Art Centre, Liverpool, UK. **1990** *Pachipamwe III*, National Gallery, Harare, Zimbabwe. **1993** *Art Sans Frontiers*, Watermans Arts Centre, London, UK. **1996** Calder Art Center, Grand Valley State University, Allendale, MI, US. **2000** Standort Gallery, Frankfurt, Germany. **2001** deliArt Gallery, London, UK. **2004** *Beyond Surface: The Sublime Picture Show*, Art in Perpetuity Trust, London, UK. **2006** *Terra Incognita*, Atelier Wilhelmina Gasthuisterrein, Amsterdam, The Netherlands. **2008** *META*, Anglia Ruskin University, Cambridge, UK. **2010** *Mix*, APT Gallery, London, UK.

Jennifer Durrant

Born 1942, Brighton, UK.
Lives and works in Umbria, Italy.
Studio at Stockwell Depot 1972–79.
Exhibited at Stockwell Depot 1976.

Selected exhibitions:
1966 *Young Contemporaries*, FBA Gallery, London, UK. **1967** Kasmin Limited, London, UK. **1967** *Survey 67*, Camden Arts Centre, London, UK. **1968** *Leicestershire Education Authority Collection Exhibition*, Whitechapel Art Gallery, London, UK. **1970** *John Moores Exhibition*, Walker Art Gallery, Liverpool, UK. **1974** *Summer Show 1*, Serpentine Gallery, London, UK. **1976** *Arts Council Collection*, Hayward Gallery, London, UK. **1977** *Twelve British Artists*, Municipal Art Gallery, Reykjavík, Iceland. **1979** *Hayward Annual*, Hayward Gallery, London, UK. **1979** *Paintings 1976–79*, Arnolfini Gallery, Bristol, UK. **1980** *The New Generation: A Curator's Choice*, André Emmerich Gallery, New York, NY, US. **1982** Carnegie International, Carnegie Institute, Pittsburgh, PA, US. **1982** *New Acquisitions*, Tate Gallery, London, UK. **1986** Northern Centre for Contemporary Art, Sunderland, UK. **1987** Serpentine Gallery, London, UK. **1988** Newlyn Orion Gallery, Penzance, UK. **1992** Concourse Gallery, Barbican Centre, London, UK. **1994** *Paint Marks*, Kettle's Yard, Cambridge, UK. **1996** Francis Graham-Dixon Gallery, London, UK. **1997** *Black, White and Colour: Works on Paper by Artists from the Royal Academy*, Sharjah Art Museum, Sharjah, United Arab Emirates. **2000** Salander-O'Reilly Galleries, New York, NY, US. **2005** Friends' Room at Royal Academy of Arts, London, UK. **2008** Art First. London, UK. **2011** Richmond Hill Gallery, London, UK.

David Evison*

Born 1944, Kwantung Province, China.
Lives and works in Beijing, China and Berlin, Germany.
Studio at Stockwell Depot 1967–93.
Exhibited at Stockwell Depot 1968–69, 1975.

Selected exhibitions:
1968 Prospect 68, Kunsthalle Düsseldorf, Dusseldorf, Germany. **1969** *New Sculpture 1969*, Arts Council touring exhibition, UK. **1970** *Stockwell Depot: Eight English Sculptors From London*, Kunstnernes Hus, Oslo, Norway and Konsthallen, Gothenburg, Sweden. **1970** Kasmin Limited, London, UK. **1970** *British Sculpture Out of the Sixties*, Institute of Contemporary Arts, London, UK. **1972** Kasmin Limited, London, UK. **1973** *The Square Collection*, Arts Council, London, UK. **1974** *British Art – The Mid-Seventies*, Jahrhunderthalle, Frankfurt, Germany. **1975** *The Condition of Sculpture*, Hayward Gallery, London, UK. **1977** Victorian Art Museum, Melbourne, Australia. **1995** Atrium Gallery, London, UK. **2006** *Sculpture and Relief*, Art Channel, Beijing, China. **2008** Galerie Gerken, Berlin, Germany. **2009** *Axis Bold as Love*, Galerie Im Regierungsviertel-Forgotten Bar, Berlin, Germany. **2010** *Sculptors: Three Generations*, Dada Post, Berlin, Germany. **2012** *Skulptur*, Galerie Gerken, Berlin, Germany. **2014** *Malerei, Zeichnung, Skulptur*, Galerie Born, Born am Darss, Germany. **2015** *Continuous Abstraction*, Galerie Nord, Berlin, Germany.

Roger Fagin*

Born 1942, South Africa.
Lives and works in France.
Studio at Stockwell Depot 1967–70.
Exhibited at Stockwell Depot 1968–69.

Selected exhibitions:
1969 *New Sculpture 1969*, Arts Council touring exhibition, UK. **1970** *Stockwell Depot: Eight English Sculptors from London*, Kunstnernes Hus, Oslo, Norway and Konsthallen, Gothenburg, Sweden. **1974** *Art Into Landscape I*, Serpentine Gallery, London, UK. **1978** *Art for Whom?*, Serpentine Gallery, London, UK.

John Foster

Born 1951, London, UK.
Died 2008, Norwich, UK.
Studio at Stockwell Depot 1971–75.
Exhibited at Stockwell Depot 1974–75, 1977–79.

Selected exhibitions:
1973 *Sculpture at Marble Hill House*, Marble Hill House, London, UK. **1979** *Summer Show 2*, Serpentine Gallery, London, UK. **1980** Narrow Street, London, UK. **1982** *Sculpture from Stockwell Depot*, Sainsbury Centre for Visual Arts, Norwich, UK. **1986** *Hardingham Sculpture Workshop*, Sainsbury Centre for Visual Arts, Norwich, UK. **1991** *Large Steel Sculptures*, Norwich Cathedral, Norwich, UK. **1995** *Ten Sculptors from the Hardingham Workshops*, Christchurch Park, Ipswich, UK. **1995** Grounds for Sculpture, Allentown, PA, US. **1995** Josine Bokhoven Gallery, Amsterdam, The Netherlands.

John Fowler*

Born 1943, Newark-on-Trent, UK.
Lives and works in London, UK.
Studio at Stockwell Depot 1968–70.
Exhibited at Stockwell Depot 1968–69.

Selected exhibitions:
1961 *Young Contemporaries*, Whitechapel Art Gallery, London, UK. **1966** *Towards Art II*, Arts Council Gallery, London, UK. **1970** *Stockwell Depot: Eight English Sculptors from London*, Kunstnernes Hus, Oslo, Norway and Konsthallen, Gothenburg, Sweden.

Gilbert & George*

Gilbert Prousch born 1943, San Martin de Tor, Italy.
George Passmore born 1942, Plymouth, UK.
Live and work in London, UK.
Studio at Stockwell Depot 1970–71.

Selected exhibitions:
1969 Stedelijk Museum, Amsterdam, The Netherlands. **1971** *Documenta 5*, Kassel, Germany. **1971** Whitechapel Art Gallery, London, UK. **1985** Solomon R Guggenheim Museum, New York, NY, US. **1987** Hayward Gallery, London, UK. **1989** Anthony d'Offay Gallery, London, UK. **1990** Central House of the Artists, Moscow, Russia. **1992** *New Democratic Pictures*, Aarhus Kunstmuseum, Aarhus, Denmark. **1993** *China Exhibition 1993*, National Art Gallery, Beijing and The Art Museum, Shanghai, China. **1994** Museo d'Arte Moderna, Lugano, Switzerland. **1997** Musée d'Art Moderne de la Ville de Paris, Paris, France. **2002** Serpentine Gallery, London, UK. **2005** Venice Biennale, Venice, Italy. **2007** Tate Modern, London, UK. **2008** Brooklyn Museum, New York, NY, US. **2011** Laznia Centre for Contemporary Art, Gdansk, Poland. **2015** *The Early Years*, Museum of Modern Art, New York, NY, US.

Katherine Gili*

Born 1948, Oxford, UK.
Lives and works in Faversham, UK.
Studio at Stockwell Depot 1973–78.
Exhibited at Stockwell Depot 1974–79.

Selected exhibitions:
1973 *Platform 73*, Museum of Modern Art, Oxford, UK. **1974** *Six Sculptors*, Chelsea Gallery, London, UK. **1975** *The Condition of Sculpture*, Hayward Gallery, London, UK. **1975** *Sculpture in a Landscape*, Marble Hill House, London, UK. **1977** *St Martin's South Bank Sculpture*, South Bank, London, UK. **1977** *Summer Exhibition 2*, Serpentine Gallery, London, UK. **1979** *Hayward Annual*, Hayward Gallery, London, UK. **1981** Salander-O'Reilly Gallery, New York, NY, US. **1982** *Sculpture from Stockwell Depot*, Sainsbury Centre for Visual Arts, Norwich, UK. **1984** *Have You Seen Sculpture from the Body?*, Tate Gallery, London, UK. **1986** *Human Interest*, Cornerhouse Gallery, Manchester, UK. **1988** *Escultura Nueva Reino Unido*, Centro Cultural del Conde Duque, Madrid, Spain. **1993** *Moving Into View*, Southbank Centre, London, UK. **1994** *Paintings by Graham Boyd, Sculptures by Katherine Gili*, Charterhouse Gallery, London, UK. **1995** *British Abstract Art: Sculpture*, Flowers East, London, UK. **1998** *British Figurative Art*, Flowers East, London, UK. **2007** *Saint Martin's Sculptors*, Poussin Gallery, London, UK. **2011** *A Career Survey*, Poussin Gallery, London, UK. **2013** *Summer Exhibition*, Royal Academy of Arts, London, UK.

John Golding

Born 1929, Hastings, UK.
Died 2012, London, UK.
Studio at Stockwell Depot c.1971–74.

Selected exhibitions:
1962 Gallery One, London, UK. **1974** *Hayward Annual*, Hayward Gallery, London, UK. **1980** *Colour in British Painting*, Hong Kong Museum of Art, Hong Kong. **1994** Mayor Gallery, London, UK. **2001** *A Cross Section through Contemporary British Art*, Ankara Art Fair, Ankara, Turkey. **1984** Annely Juda Fine Art, London, UK. **2003** New Art Centre, Salisbury, UK. **2004** *Making Things Public*, Witte de With Centre for Contemporary Art, Rotterdam, The Netherlands. **2010** Tate Britain, London, UK. **2011** *Artists for Kettle's Yard*, Kettle's Yard, Cambridge, UK. **2012** Annely Juda Fine Art, London, UK. **2014** *Abstract Drawing*, Drawing Room, London, UK. **2015** *Abstraction and the Art of John Golding*, Sainsbury Centre for Visual Arts, Norwich, UK.

Alan Gouk

Born 1939, Belfast, UK.
Lives and works in London and Montrose, UK.
Exhibited at Stockwell Depot 1975–79.

Selected exhibitions:
1967 *John Moores Exhibition*, Liverpool, UK. **1968** *Preview-London*, Camden Arts Centre, London, UK. **1970** *Nine Painters*, Hayward Gallery, London, UK. **1971** Museum of Modern Art, Oxford, UK. **1972** Hayward Gallery, London, UK. **1977** *Four Abstract Artists*, Fruitmarket Gallery, Edinburgh, UK. **1979** *Two from Stockwell*, City Art Gallery, Leeds, UK. **1982** Woodlands Gallery, London, UK. **1986** Smith's Gallery, London, UK. **1989** *Scottish Painting since 1900*, Scottish National Gallery of Modern Art, Edinburgh, UK. **1990** *Colour in Modern Painting*, Stoke City Museum and Art Gallery, UK. **1993** *British Painterly Abstraction*, Tate Gallery, London, UK. **1995** *British Abstract Art, Part I: Paintings*, Flowers East, London, UK. **1995** *The St Cyrus Series*, Flowers East, London, UK. **2000** *30th Anniversary Exhibition*, Flowers East, London, UK. **2002** *John Moores Exhibition*, Walker Art Gallery, Liverpool, UK. **2005** *Mainstream Abstract Painting from the Seventies*, Poussin Gallery, London, UK. **2007** *The Ulysses Series*, Poussin Gallery, London, UK. **2008** *Poussin Review 2008: Form and Space*, Poussin Gallery, London, UK. **2012** *New Paintings*, Poussin Gallery, London, UK. **2014** *New Small Paintings*, Hampstead School of Art Gallery, London, UK.

Gerard Hemsworth*

Born 1945, London, UK.
Lives and works in Hastings, UK.
Studio at Stockwell Depot 1967–70.
Exhibited at Stockwell Depot 1968–69.

Selected exhibitions:
1965 AIA Gallery, London, UK. **1966** *New Dimensions*, Camden Art Centre, London, UK. **1967** *Six Young Artists*, Institute of Contemporary Art, London, UK. **1967** *Young Contemporaries*, Tate Gallery, London, UK. **1969** *New Sculpture 1969*, Arts Council touring exhibition, UK. **1970** *Stockwell Depot: Eight English Sculptors from London*, Kunstnernes Hus, Oslo, Norway and Konsthallen, Gothenburg, Sweden. **1970** *British Sculpture Out of the Sixties*, Institute of Contemporary Arts, London. **1970** Nigel Greenwood Gallery, London, UK. **1972** *Presenting Things as They Are*, Museum of Modern Art, Oxford, UK. **1976** Carlisle Museum and Art Gallery, Carlisle, UK. **1977** *Ten White Paintings*, Oliver Dowling Gallery, Dublin, Ireland. **1980** *Object/Nature – Still Life Drawing*, Piwna 20/26, Warsaw, Poland. **1981** International Cultureel Centrum, Antwerp, Belgium. **1982** *Art and the Sea*, Institute of Contemporary Art, London, UK. **1984** Third Eye Centre, Glasgow, UK. **1985** Galerie Van Beveren, Rotterdam, The Netherlands. **1987** Tony Shafrazi Gallery, New York, NY, US. **1989** *Financial Times*, Anthony Reynolds Gallery, London, UK. **1998** *Strictly Suburban*, John Hansard Gallery, Southampton, UK. **2002** Thomas Cohn Galeria, São Paulo, Brazil. **2006** *John Moores Exhibition*, Walker Art Gallery, Liverpool, UK. **2009** *Hidden Agenda*, Aldrich Contemporary Art Museum, Ridgefield, CT, US. **2010** *Use & Mention*, Stephen Lawrence Gallery, University of Greenwich, London, UK. **2015** *Outing*, Thomas Rehbein Galerie, Cologne, Germany.

Peter Hide*

Born 1944, Carshalton, UK.
Lives and works in Edmonton, Canada.
Studio at Stockwell Depot 1967–86.
Exhibited at Stockwell Depot 1968–79.

Selected exhibitions:
1966 Grabowski Gallery, London, UK. **1968** *Survey 68*, Camden Arts Centre, London, UK. **1968** Prospect 68, Kunsthalle Düsseldorf, Dusseldorf, Germany. **1969** *New Sculpture 1969*, Arts Council touring exhibition, UK. **1970** *Stockwell Depot: Eight English Sculptors from London*, Kunstnernes Hus, Oslo, Norway and Konsthallen, Gothenburg, Sweden. **1970** *Some Recent Art in Britain*, Leeds City Art Gallery, Leeds, UK. **1973** *Sculpture at Marble Hill House*, Marble Hill House, London, UK. **1975** *The Condition of Sculpture*, Hayward Gallery, London, UK. **1976** Serpentine Gallery, London, UK. **1977** *Queen's Silver Jubilee Exhibition*, Battersea Park, London, UK. **1979** Arnolfini Gallery, Bristol, UK. **1980** *Alberta Now*, Edmonton Art Gallery, Edmonton, Canada. **1982** *Sculpture from Stockwell Depot*, Sainsbury Centre for Visual Arts, Norwich, UK. **1986** *Triangle UK*, Smith's Gallery, London, UK. **1989** *New Acquisitions*, Tate Gallery, London, UK. **1990** *Monumental Sculptures*, André Emmerich Gallery, New York, NY, US. **1992** *New Displays*, Tate Gallery, London, UK. **1998** *Peter Hide In Context*, Edmonton Art Gallery, Edmonton, Canada. **2003** *New Small Sculpture*, Scott Gallery, Edmonton, Canada. **2003** *Monumental Sculpture*, Jesus College, University of Cambridge, Cambridge, UK. **2007** *Sculpture*, Poussin Gallery, London, UK. **2008** Royal Alberta Museum, Edmonton, Canada. **2011** *United Enemies: The Problem of Sculpture in Britain in the 1960s and 1970s*, Henry Moore Institute, Leeds, UK. **2012** *Seven Years in the City*, Art Gallery of Alberta, Edmonton, Canada. **2013** *Protesting Time*, Piper Gallery, London, UK.

Geoff Hollow

Born 1944, London, UK.
Died 1998, London, UK.
Studio at Stockwell Depot 1974–83.
Exhibited at Stockwell Depot 1979.

Selected exhibitions:
1977 *Whitechapel Open*, Whitechapel Art Gallery, London, UK. **1981** Air Gallery, London, UK. **1985** *Marilyn Hallam, Geoff Hollow and Paul Tonkin: New Paintings*, Castlefield Gallery, Manchester, UK. **1988** Wolfson College, University of Oxford, Oxford, UK. **1989** Greenwich Theatre Gallery, London, UK. **1990** Sandra Higgins Fine Art, London, UK. **1992** Kepler Gallery, London, UK. **1992** Works Gallery, New York, NY, US. **1993** City Museum & Art Gallery, Hanley, UK. **1993** Woodlands Art Gallery, London, UK. **1994** *Made in Greenwich*, The Living Room, London, UK. **1999** Workplace Gallery, London, UK. **2006** *Direct Colour*, Poussin Gallery, London, UK. **2007** *Poussin Review: Recent British Abstract Painting and Sculpture*, Poussin Gallery, London, UK.

Richard James

Born 1937, Thorne, UK.
Lives and works in Norwich, UK.
Studio at Stockwell Depot c.1971–74.
Exhibited at Stockwell Depot 1972–73.

Selected exhibitions:
1973 *Painting* 3, Serpentine Gallery, London, UK. **1974** *John Moores Exhibition*, Walker Art Centre, Liverpool, UK. **1974** *British Painting 74*, Hayward Gallery, London, UK. **1977** *British Painting 1952–1977*, Royal Academy of Arts, London, UK. **1980** *Hayward Annual*, Hayward Gallery, London, UK. **1981** Gallery 49, Norwich, UK. **1992** Beardsmore Gallery, London, UK.

Roelof Louw*

Born 1935, Cape Town, South Africa.
Lives and works in Cape Town, South Africa.
Studio at Stockwell Depot 1967–70.
Exhibited at Stockwell Depot 1968–69.

Selected exhibitions:
1964 *Young Contemporaries*, London, UK. **1967** Kasmin Limited, London, UK. **1968** *Survey 68*, Camden Arts Centre, London, UK. **1969** *Location*, Museum of Modern Art, Oxford, UK. **1969** *Op Losse Schroeven*, Stedelijk Museum, Amsterdam, The Netherlands. **1969** *557,087*, Seattle Art Museum, Seattle, WA, US. **1969** *String and Rope*, Sidney Janis Gallery, New York, NY, US. **1969** *Interventions*, Le Centre National d'Art Contemporain, Paris, France. **1969** *When Attitudes Become Form*, Kunsthalle Bern, Bern, Switzerland and Institute of Contemporary Arts, London. **1969** *New Sculpture 1969*, Arts Council touring exhibition, UK. **1970** *Stockwell Depot: Eight English Sculptors from London*, Kunstnernes Hus, Oslo, Norway and Konsthallen, Gothenburg, Sweden. **1970** *Wall Show*, Lisson Gallery, London, UK. **1970** *Between Man and Matter*, Tokyo Biennale, Tokyo, Japan. **1970** *British Sculpture Out of the Sixties*, Institute of Contemporary Arts, London. **1971** *Tape Recorder Project*, Whitechapel Art Gallery, London, UK. **1971** *The British Avant-Garde*, New York Cultural Centre, New York, NY, US. **1976** *3 Sculptors*, Fine Arts Building, New York, NY, US. **1980** *Drawings/Public Places*, Massachusetts Institute of Technology, Cambridge, MA, US. **1980** *Drawings/Structures*, Institute of Contemporary Art, Boston, MA, US. **1998** Hanël Gallery, Cape Town, South Africa. **2000** *Live in Your Head*, Whitechapel Gallery, London, UK. **2004** *Hellfire*, NSA Gallery, Durban, South Africa. **2013** *Rolled Lead Piece (1970)*, Karsten Schubert, London, UK. **2014** *Holland Park (1967)*, Frieze Sculpture Park, London, UK.

John McLean

Born 1939, Liverpool, UK.
Lives and works in London, UK.
Studio at Stockwell Depot 1969–93.
Exhibited at Stockwell Depot 1975–77, 1979.

Selected exhibitions:
1963 AIA Gallery, London, UK. **1966** McRoberts & Tunnard, London, UK. **1967** Axiom Gallery, London, UK. **1967** Museum of Modern Art, Oxford, UK. **1970** London Group, London, UK. **1971** *Big Paintings for Public Places*, Whitworth Art Gallery, Manchester, UK. **1971** *Summer Show 5: Cézanne is the father of modern painting*, Serpentine Gallery, London, UK. **1974** *British Painting 74*, Hayward Gallery, London, UK. **1975** Talbot Rice Gallery, University of Edinburgh, Edinburgh, UK. **1975** *New Work*, Hayward Gallery, London, UK. **1977** *Four Abstract Artists*, Fruitmarket Gallery, Edinburgh, UK. **1978** House Gallery, London, UK. **1979** *The British Art Show*, Mappin Art Gallery, Sheffield, UK. **1980** Nicola Jacobs Gallery, London, UK. **1982** Artspace Galleries, Aberdeen, UK. **1984** Mark Gerrard Gallery, Edmonton, Canada. **1988** Kapil Jariwala, New York, NY, US. **1994** *Paint Marks*, Southampton City Art Gallery, Southampton, UK. **1994** Francis Graham-Dixon Gallery, London, UK. **1999** Flowers East, London, UK. **2003** Talbot Rice Gallery, University of Edinburgh, Edinburgh, UK. **2007** Poussin Gallery, London, UK. **2008** Cross Street Gallery, London, UK. **2009** Broadbent, London, UK. **2013** *Another Light: Prairie Journey*, Fine Art Society, London, UK.

Mali Morris

Born 1945, North Wales, UK.
Lives and works in London, UK.
Exhibited at Stockwell Depot 1979.

Selected exhibitions:
1967 *Northern Young Contemporaries*, Newcastle upon Tyne, UK. **1968** *London Group*, RI Galleries, London, UK. **1972** *Road Show*, São Paulo, Brazil. **1974** SPACE, London, UK. **1977** *Summer Show 3*, Serpentine Gallery, London, UK. **1978** *Drawing in Action*, Ferens Art Gallery, Hull, UK. **1979** Ikon Gallery, Birmingham, UK. **2000** *Mali Morris and Alexis Harding*, Pump House Gallery, London, UK. **2002** *John Moores Exhibition*, Walker Art Gallery, Liverpool, UK. **2002** Angel Row Gallery, Nottingham, UK. **2005** *Work from Four Decades*, Poussin Gallery, London, UK. **2005** Robert Steele Gallery Project Room, New York, NY, US. **2010** Royal Academy of Arts, London, UK. **2010** The Cut Gallery, Halesworth, Suffolk, UK. **2011** *Uncaught Hares*, Stephen Lawrence Gallery, University of Greenwich, London, UK. **2012** *Finger*, Hidde van Seggelen Gallery, London, UK. **2012** *Works on Canvas and Paper*, Mostyn Gallery, Llandudno, UK. **2013** *Pop and Abstract*, National Museum Wales, Cardiff, UK. **2014** *As Exciting as We Can Make It: Ikon in the 1980s*, Ikon Gallery, Birmingham, UK.

Robert Persey*

Born 1951, London, UK.
Lives and works in Kent, UK.
Studio at Stockwell Depot 1977.
Exhibited at Stockwell Depot 1979.

Selected exhibitions:
1977 *New Contemporaries*, Royal Academy of Arts, London, UK. **1977** *Saint Martin's South Bank Sculpture*, South Bank, London, UK. **1980** *Painting and Sculpture at Roehampton Institute*, Roehampton Institute, London, UK. **1983** *Sculpture from the Body*, Woodlands Art Gallery, London, UK. **1984** *Have You Seen Sculpture from the Body?*, Tate Gallery, London, UK. **1986** *Ten Graduates Show*, Saint Martin's School of Art, London, UK. **1987** *An Exhibition of Sculpture*, Whitefriars Museum, Coventry, UK. **1988** *Esultura Nueva Reino Unido*, Centro Cultural del Conde Duque, Madrid, Spain. **1992** *Painters and Sculptors from the Greenwich Studios*, Woodlands Art Gallery, London, UK. **1993** Lanchester Gallery, Coventry, UK. **1994** Exhibition Gallery, Milton Keynes, UK. **1994** *Made in Greenwich 1974–94*, Living Room Gallery, London, UK. **1996** *Class Act*, Woodlands Art Gallery, London, UK. **2003** *Blok Sculpture Festival*, Canterbury, UK. **2003** Cork Street Gallery, London, UK. **2011** *Uncaught Hares*, Stephen Lawrence Gallery, University of Greenwich, London, UK.

Fred Pollock

Born 1937, Glasgow, UK.
Lives and works in London, UK.
Exhibited at Stockwell Depot 1975–79.

Selected exhibitions:
1963 New Charing Cross Gallery, Glasgow, UK. **1968** *Preview-London*, Camden Art Centre, London, UK. **1974** Garage Gallery, London, UK. **1975** *Choice Selection*, Fruitmarket Gallery, Edinburgh, UK. **1977** *British Painting 1952–1977*, Royal Academy of Arts, London, UK. **1977** *Four Abstract Artists*, Fruitmarket Gallery, Edinburgh, UK. **1980** *Hayward Annual*, Hayward Gallery, London, UK. **1982** Serpentine Gallery, London, UK. **1986** Vanessa Devereux Gallery, London, UK. **1993** Talbot Rice Gallery, University of Edinburgh, Edinburgh, UK. **1994** Rebecca Hossack Gallery, London, UK. **2005** Poussin Gallery, London, UK. **2008** *A Career Survey*, Poussin Gallery, London, UK. **2011** *High-Abstract*, Poussin Gallery, London, UK.

Geoff Rigden

Born 1943, Cheltenham, UK.
Lives and works in London, UK.
Exhibited at Stockwell Depot 1975, 1979.

Selected exhibitions:
1965 *Young Contemporaries*, London, UK. **1965** *John Moores Exhibition*, Walker Art Gallery, Liverpool, UK. **1968** AIA Gallery, London, UK. **1968** *Preview-London*, Camden Art Centre, London, UK. **1968** *New Work*, Leeds Institute Gallery, Leeds, UK. **1971** Museum of Modern Art, Oxford, UK. **1977** Tolly Cobbold/Eastern Arts Association, London, UK. **1977** Zygos Gallery, Nicosia, Cyprus. **1979** *Summer Show 2*, Serpentine Gallery, London, UK. **1980** *Hayward Annual*, Hayward Gallery, London, UK. **1982** Spacex Gallery, Exeter, UK. **1983** Air Gallery, London, UK. **1988** Francis Graham-Dixon Gallery, London, UK. **1989** *Whitechapel Open*, Whitechapel Art Gallery, London, UK. **1990** *Colour in Modern Painting*, City Art Gallery, Stoke-on-Trent, UK. **1995** Francis Graham-Dixon Gallery, London, UK. **2001** *British Abstract Painting*, Flowers East, London, UK. **2002** *John Moores Exhibition*, Walker Art Gallery, Liverpool, UK. **2005** *Mainstream Abstract Painting from the Seventies*, Poussin Gallery, London, UK. **2008** *Summer Exhibition*, Royal Academy of Arts, London, UK. **2009** *The Seamless Garment*, Broadbent Gallery, London, UK. **2012** *Paintings and Constructions: 1972–2012*, Poussin Gallery, London, UK. **2012** *Double Vision*, The Lion and Lamb Gallery, London, UK.

Mark Skilton*

Born 1954, London, UK.
Lives and works in Bath, UK.
Studio at Stockwell Depot 1977–83.
Exhibited at Stockwell Depot 1979.

Selected exhibitions:
1977 *New Contemporaries*, Royal Academy of Arts, London, UK. **1977** *Saint Martin's South Bank Sculpture*, South Bank, London, UK. **1979** Cannizaro Park, London, UK. **1984** *Have You Seen Sculpture from the Body?*, Tate Gallery, London, UK. **2010** *Poussin Review 2010: New to Sight*, Poussin Gallery, London, UK.

Anthony Smart*

Born 1949, Hull, UK.
Lives and works near King's Lynn, UK.
Studio at Stockwell Depot 1973–75.
Exhibited at Stockwell Depot 1974–79.

Selected exhibitions:
1972 *Platform 72*, Museum of Modern Art, Oxford, UK. **1975** *The Condition of Sculpture*, Hayward Gallery, London, UK. **1975** *Sculpture at Greenwich*, London, UK. **1977** *Queen's Silver Jubilee Exhibition*, Battersea Park, London, UK. **1977** *Microcosm: Maquettes, Drawings and Related Material*, Redfern Gallery, London, UK. **1977** *Saint Martin's South Bank Sculpture*, London, UK. **1979** *Style in the Seventies*, Arnolfini Gallery, Bristol, UK. **1982** *Sculpture from Stockwell Depot*, Sainsbury Centre for Visual Arts, Norwich, UK. **1984** *Have You Seen Sculpture from the Body?*, Tate Gallery, London, UK. **1988** *Escultura Nueva Reino Unido*, Centro Cultural del Conde Duque, Madrid, Spain. **2007** *Saint Martin's Sculpture*, Poussin Gallery, London, UK. **2009** Poussin Gallery, London, UK.

Paul Tonkin

Born 1951, Southampton, UK.
Lives and works in London, UK.
Exhibited at Stockwell Depot 1976–79.

Selected exhibitions:
1974 Stockwell Public Library, London, UK. **1980** Air Gallery, London, UK. **1980** *Hayward Annual*, Hayward Gallery, London, UK. **1982** *Summer Show 3*, Serpentine Gallery, London, UK. **1984** *Whitechapel Open*, Whitechapel Art Gallery, London, UK. **1985** *Marilyn Hallam, Geoff Hollow and Paul Tonkin*, Castlefield Gallery, Manchester, UK. **1989** Merz Gallery, Edinburgh, UK. **2006** *Poussin Review 2006: Recent British Abstract Painting and Sculpture*, Poussin Gallery, London, UK. **2009** Poussin Gallery, London, UK. **2010** *Mix*, APT Gallery, London, UK. **2011** *Uncaught Hares*, Stephen Lawrence Gallery, University of Greenwich, London, UK.

Gary Wragg

Born 1946, High Wycombe, UK.
Lives and works in London, UK.
Studio at Stockwell Depot 1968–69.

Selected exhibitions:
1969 *Play Orbit*, Institute of Contemporary Art, London, UK. **1971** *Platform 71*, Museum of Modern Art, Oxford, UK. **1971** *Young Contemporaries*, Royal Academy of Arts, London, UK. **1972** *Drawing*, Museum of Modern Art, Oxford, UK. **1974** *British Painting 1974*, Hayward Gallery, London, UK. **1976** Acme Gallery, London, UK. **1977** *British Painting 1952–1977*, Royal Academy of Arts, London, UK. **1984** *English Expressionism*, Warwick Arts Centre, Coventry, UK. **1985** *30 London Painters*, Royal Academy of Arts, London, UK. **1987** *Retrospective*, Castlefield Gallery, Manchester, UK. **1991** *John Moores Exhibition*, Walker Art Gallery, Liverpool, UK. **1992** *London Group*, Concourse Gallery, Barbican Centre, London, UK. **1997** Flowers East, London, UK. **2004** *Wragg and McLean*, Vinopolis, London, UK. **2008** *Four Abstract Artists*, Flowers, London, UK. **2010** *Early Works 1968–1969*, Alan Wheatley Art, London, UK. **2012** *Spontaneity of Movements*, Alan Wheatley Art, London, UK. **2014** *Constant Within The Change*, Clifford Chance, London, UK.

Acknowledgements

I would like to thank all the artists who showed or worked at Stockwell Depot and who helped with my research: Douglas Abercrombie, David Annesley, Stephenie Bergman, Mick Blake, Shirley Cameron, Tim Coppard, Jeff Dellow, Jennifer Durrant, David Evison, Roger Fagin, John Fowler, Gilbert & George, Katherine Gili, Alan Gouk, Eddy Hemsley, Gerard Hemsworth, Peter Hide, Roelof Louw, Barry Martin, John McLean, Mali Morris, Robert Persey, Fred Pollock, Geoff Rigden, Kay Saunders, Mark Skilton, Anthony Smart, Cheron Tomkins, Paul Tonkin and Gary Wragg.

Special thanks to Robin Greenwood for his work with Poussin Gallery, where my interest in Stockwell Depot started; Jon Wood of the Henry Moore Institute for his preface; and Bill Linskey, chair of the Brixton Historical Society for generously sharing his research on the early history of the Depot. Thanks are also due to David Anfam, Ray Barrie, Frank Bowling, Samantha Blake of the BBC, Pam Brown, James Faure-Walker, Dama Hanks, Steve Lewis, Jeff Lowe, Michael Lyons, Gina Medcalf, Piano Nobile, Sean Pollock, Ray Sacks, Tim Scott, Veronica Sekules of the Sainsbury Centre for the Visual Arts, Richard Siemens, Joy Sleeman, Anne Smart, Mary Sykes and Ben Wiedel-Kaufmann.

This book would not have been possible without the support of Jim Cockburn and John Pluthero. The project has also been very generously supported by Arts Council England, Henry Moore Foundation and the Paul Mellon Centre for Studies in British Art. My research would not have been possible without the assistance of the staff of the Tate Library and Archive, the Henry Moore Institute, the Arts Council Collection and the Victoria and Albert Museum Archives. Finally my thanks to Karsten Schubert, Doro Globus, Louisa Green, Daniel Griffiths and Jay Drinkall at Ridinghouse; University of Greenwich Galleries and their curator, David Waterworth; Richard Deal at Dexter Premedia; Eileen Daly, Dorothy Feaver, Ann Hale and Mark Thomson for their contributions to the publication.

Credits

Image credits

© Peter Hide: pp.10–11, 41 (bottom), 51, 75–77, 83, 87–90, 102, 111, 117, 135, 143
© The Estate of Charles Harrison: pp.10–11
Courtesy Collection of Bill Linskey: pp.15 (top), 22
© David Evison: pp.15 (bottom left), 41 (top), 48, 55, 73, 82, 95 (bottom), 100, 105, 118, 127 (top)
© Katherine Gili: pp.15 (right), 94, 97, 106, 113, 126, 133, 139
Courtesy Conway Library, The Courtauld Institute of Art, London: pp.20–21, 112
© Gilbert & George: p.27 (bottom)
Courtesy of Arnolfini Gallery, Bristol: p.34 (top)
Courtesy Mark Skilton: p.34 (bottom left)
Original photography by Nicholas Mackenzie and poster design by Nigel Hall: p.34 (right)
Courtesy Sainsbury Centre for Visual Arts, University of East Anglia: p.39
© Roelof Louw: pp.45, 57, 58 (top)
© 2015 Roland Brener. All rights reserved: pp.46–47, 58 (bottom), 64, 67, 69, 72
© Tate, London 2015: pp.49, 52 (bottom), 60–61, 70–71
© Shirley Cameron 1967: p.53
© John McLean. All Rights Reserved, DACS 2015: pp.62, 78, 81, 101, 151
© Gary Wragg: p.63
© Victoria and Albert Museum, London: p.65
Courtesy of the Architects' Journal: pp.76–77
© John Golding Artistic Trust. Courtesy Annely Juda Fine Art, London: p.79
© John Foster Estate: pp.85–86, 91–92, 108, 122, 131, 138
© Anthony Smart: pp.93, 95 (top), 107, 114–15, 123, 132, 137
© Fred Pollock: pp.98, 125, 147
© Alan Gouk: pp.103, 121, 134, 140
© Stephenie Bergman: p.104
Courtesy of the Whitworth, The University of Manchester: p.105
© G R 2015: pp.109, 150
© Jennifer Durrant: p.116
© Paul Tonkin: pp.119, 124
© Douglas Abercrombie: pp.129, 146
© Mark Skilton: p.141
© Robert Persey: p.142
© Mali Morris: p.144
© Jeff Dellow: p.145
© Estate of Geoffrey Hollow: p.148
Courtesy of the artist and Arnolfini Gallery, Bristol: p.149

Photography credits

Ray Sacks: pp.2–3, 6, 27 (top), 56–57, 59, 64, 68, 69 (top), 152–53, 164–65
The Courtauld Institute of Art, London: pp.20–21, 112
Jem Southam: p.34 (top), 149
Dexter Premedia, London: p.34 (right)
Richard Siemens: pp.41 (bottom), 135, 143
Roland Brener: pp.47, 58 (bottom), 67, 69 (bottom), 72
J L Nelson: p.49
© 1970 Andrew Dunlop: p.50
Shirley Cameron: p.53
Paul Tucker: p.63
Antonica Photos: p.75
Andy Phillipson: pp.78, 81
G W Hide: p.90
Peter Barron: pp.93, 95 (top)
Carlos Granger: pp.94, 102, 122–23
Chris Killip: p.95 (bottom)
Katherine Gili: pp.97, 106, 113, 126, 133, 142
Paul Minyo: pp.98, 103, 119, 124–25, 129, 146–47
Peter Chadwick: p.130
Positive Image Photography: pp.134, 140
Orlando Gili: p.139
Mark Skilton: p.141
Jeff Dellow: p.145
Nicholas Mackenzie: front cover

Collection credits

Collection Gillian Ayres: p.41 (top)
Collections of the respective artists: pp.41 (bottom), 48, 63, 89, 94 (bottom), 95 (bottom), 97–98, 103, 109, 116–17, 119, 124–125, 127–29, 133–34, 139–44, 146–47
Gift of Mrs Joseph Halle Schaffner, through UCSB Art Affiliates, Art, Design & Architecture Museum, UC Santa Barbara: p.47
Arts Council Collection, Southbank Centre, London: pp.62, 101, 104, 123
Private collection: p.73
The University of Edinburgh Art Collection: pp.78, 81
Gilder Lehrman Collection: p.87
Collection Hilary Prince: p.90
Private collection: p.102
The Whitworth, The University of Manchester: p.105
Private collection, UK: p.106
Private collection, Edmonton, Alberta: p.111
Private collection, UK: p.113
The Highland Council Collection, SAC Bequest: p.121
Private collection, UK: p.126 (left)
Collection of Mali Morris: p.150
Courtesy the British Council Collection: p.151

Great care has been taken to identify all image copyright holders correctly. In cases of errors or omissions please contact the publishers so that we can make corrections in future editions.

Published in 2015 by **Ridinghouse**
in association with the University of Greenwich

On the occasion of
Stockwell Depot 1967–79
24 July – 12 September 2015

University of Greenwich Galleries
University of Greenwich
The Old Royal Navy College
Greenwich
London SE10 9LS
United Kingdom
greenwichunigalleries.co.uk

Curator of Galleries: David Waterworth

Ridinghouse
46 Lexington Street
London W1F OLP
United Kingdom
ridinghouse.co.uk

Publisher: Doro Globus
Publishing Manager: Louisa Green
Publishing Assistant: Daniel Griffiths
Intern: Jay Drinkall

Distributed in the UK and Europe by
Cornerhouse Publications
c/o Home
2 Tony Wilson Place
Manchester M15 4FN
United Kingdom
cornerhousepublications.org

Distributed in the US by
RAM Publications + Distribution, Inc.
2525 Michigan Avenue Building A2
Santa Monica, CA 90404
United States
rampub.com

Edited by Sam Cornish, Louisa Green and David Waterworth
Copyedited by Eileen Daly
Proofread by Dorothy Feaver
Biographical research by Ann Hale
Reprographics by Dexter Premedia

Designed by Mark Thomson
Set in Haultin and Fakt
Printed in Latvia by Livoniaprint

ISBN 978 1 909932 05 0

British Library Cataloguing-in-Publication Data:
A full catalogue record of this book is available from the British Library

Supported using public funding by
ARTS COUNCIL ENGLAND
LOTTERY FUNDED

The Henry Moore Foundation

PAUL MELLON CENTRE
for Studies in British Art

UNIVERSITY of GREENWICH

Ridinghouse

Front cover:
Exterior of Stockwell Depot, London, 1976

Back cover:
Installation view, *Stockwell Depot: Studio Exhibition; New Painting and Sculpture*, Stockwell Depot, London, 1975

Left to right:
Katherine Gili, *Vertical IV* (1975); John Foster, *Three Cornered* (1975); Anthony Smart, *Roos* (1975); and Gili, *Vertical III* (1975)